INTRODUCTION

Of all the areas of law which a manager or owner in the hospitality industry will have to deal with, employment law is probably the most complex. Just over 30 years ago there was very little statute law (written law passed by Parliament) concerning employment; most of the employment relationship depended upon the common law of contract. This made it very difficult for employees to seek the protection of the law, not only because of the very high costs involved but also because the common law offered little protection to the servant, as employees were known.

The position today is fundamentally different as statute governs almost every aspect of the employment relationship. Statutory rights are enforced through industrial tribunals which provide a speedy, accessible and low-cost forum, offering a remedy of reinstatement as well as damages.

This pocket book sets out to answer a range of the key employment law questions that the owner or manager of a hotel, catering or similar business may have to answer. It could be said that employment law is the same for all businesses — of course, this is generally true. However, catering and all the related sectors of the hospitality industry have certain features which bring particular aspects of employment law to the fore. The seasonal nature and irregular hours of many catering and hotel operations as well as the mobile nature of many of the industry's workers create plenty of opportunities for legal misunderstanding about the nature of employers' and employees' rights and duties.

The book has been organised to correspond with the way that many personnel and human resource managers regard the employment relationship, ie from the metaphorical "cradle to the grave", or from the start of employment through to the end. Inevitably, there is some overlap between the various chapters but attempts have been made to keep any repetition to a minimum.

The authors are aware that in setting out to produce a concise summary, some aspects of the employment relationship may have been omitted or explained very simply. This is unavoidable in a brief book of this nature. However, more detailed information can be found in the associated works: *Croner's Catering* and *Croner's Catering Records and Procedures*. For those seeking an even deeper explanation and understanding of employment law, *Croner's Reference Book for Employers* and *Croner's Employment Law* will prove invaluable.

This book is intended as a *guide* and it is important to remember that no two cases are identical. Before taking any action, eg dismissing a long-serving employee, which may have legal consequences for you or your organisation, you should take professional legal advice.

Catering Questions & Answers: Employment Law

Michael J Boella, Marilyn Calabrese,
Clifford Goodwin, Steven Goss-Turner

Croner Publications Ltd
Croner House
London Road
Kingston upon Thames
Surrey KT2 6SR
Telephone: 0181-547 3333

THE AUTHORS

MICHAEL J BOELLA, MA, MIPD, MHCIMA, co-ordinating editor and contributor. Michael is a principal lecturer at the University of Brighton Business School where he specialises in teaching Hotel and Catering Studies. He was previously employed by Forte plc and Bass plc in personnel management roles and by Price Waterhouse as a management consultant. He is advisory editor of *Croner's Catering*.

MARILYN CALABRESE, MIPD, is a section editor of *Croner's Catering Records and Procedures* and *Croner's Caterer's Briefing*, specialising in employment matters. Marilyn is a freelance human resource consultant and teacher of Human Resource Management at the Universities of Brighton and Leicester. She previously worked for the Hotel and Catering Training Company as a training advisor and for J Lyons Catering as a personnel manager at their Gatwick Airport and City Airport catering outlets. Marilyn recently revised the hotel and catering course offered by the International Correspondence School.

CLIFFORD GOODWIN is a section editor of *Croner's Catering Records and Procedures* and an original contributor to *Croner's Management of Public Houses*. Clifford is a senior lecturer at the University of Brighton and a consultant specialising in Human Resource and Operations Management. His consultancy activities have focused on issues relating to the transfer of undertakings as a result of compulsory competitive tendering. Clifford is also a moderator for the HCIMA Diploma programme.

STEVEN GOSS-TURNER is a section editor of *Croner's Caterer's Briefing*. He is also a senior lecturer in the Department of Service Sector Management, part of the University of Brighton. Before embarking on a teaching career in 1991, he had been Training Director for the London and International division of Forte Hotels, a company with which he was associated for 15 years. Steven is author of *Managing People in the Hotel and Catering Industry*, published by Croner in 1992.

THE REVIEWERS

HELEN J DESMOND, LLB, LLM, is Lecturer in Law and Course Director, LLB by Part-time Studies, at the University of Buckingham.

ALAN MAKINSON, FHCIMA, MITD CERT ED (Leeds) is Director of Personnel and Training for DeVere Hotels Ltd, a part of the Greenall Group plc. He is a past secretary and chairman of the Hotel Employers Group for the UK and a current member of both the Industry Occupational Standards Committee and the British Hospitality Association Employment Committee.

JOHN STALLWORTHY, MBII FIPD, is a human resource consultant who has been head of personnel departments in a number of major international companies.

QUESTIONS

1. RECRUITMENT

Q1.1   What are the advantages of requiring job candidates to complete an application form?

Q1.2   Is the application form a legally binding document?

Q1.3   When designing the application form may I ask questions about the number and ages of dependants the applicant may have?

Q1.4   Am I allowed to ask for a photograph?

Q1.5   What records must I keep for the selection of a candidate?

Q1.6   At what point in the recruitment process may I apply for references?

Q1.7   Is there any limitation on the questions I can ask in a reference application?

Q1.8   If an employee has been convicted of a criminal offence in the past, what rights do I have as an employer to have access to this information?

Q1.9   Are there any legal obligations to advertise internally and externally for vacancies that occur?

Q1.10   More than 50% of the workforce in my organisation is female but there is only one female manager out of six. Are we breaking the law?

Q1.11   Are there any circumstances under which I can specify that I want to employ a man or a woman?

Q1.12   During interviews I need to ascertain the candidates' ability to attend work without having too many domestic problems such as responsibilities for children. How can I find out what I need to know without being discriminatory?

Q1.13   What does indirect discrimination mean as far as race or nationality is concerned?

Q1.14   Are there any circumstances under which I can specify that I want to employ a particular nationality or race?

Q1.15   Can I legally discriminate against a person whose religious activities require him or her to attend certain services and festivals, etc which conflict with work requirements?

Q1.16   Is there a minimum size of organisation below which sex and race discrimination legislation does not apply?

Q1.17   Are there any discriminatory implications of using psychometric tests as part of the selection process?

Q1.18   We have a predominantly young workforce. Am I legally permitted to stipulate an age limit when recruiting employees?

Q1.19   What are my obligations regarding the employment of disabled persons?

Q1.20   What restrictions are there for the employment of persons under the age of 18 within the catering industry?

Q1.21   What permits are required for potential employees from within and outside the European Union (EU)?

2. CONTRACTS

Q2.1   What are my general duties as an employer towards my employees?

Q2.2   What are the general duties owed by an employee to his or her employer?

Q2.3   How can I distinguish between an employee and a subcontractor such as a gardener, a window cleaner or even a home worker who works for me?

Q2.4   If I employ staff from an agency are they employees of our organisation?

Q2.5   How can I distinguish between a full-time employee and a part-time employee?

Q2.6   How can I distinguish between a part-time employee and a casual worker?

Q2.7   Is it important to be able to make distinctions between types of employee?

Q2.8   What constitutes a contract of employment?

Q2.9   Do contracts of employment have to be in writing?

Q2.10   Does the written statement of terms and conditions as required by the **Employment Protection (Consolidation) Act 1978** constitute a contract of employment for legal purposes?

Q2.11   When does the written statement of terms and conditions, as required by the **Employment Protection (Consolidation) Act 1978**, have to be given to an employee?

Q2.12   Am I free to negotiate any conditions into a contract?

Q2.13   How specific can I be in applying standards required for dress code, wearing jewellery and appearance, etc?

Q2.14   What has to be specified in a contract?

Q2.15   Can other documents be incorporated into a contract?

Q2.16   Does the law specify any minimum or maximum conditions in employment contracts such as pay, hours of work, holidays and sick pay, etc?

Q2.17   How can I change the conditions of employment of my employees?

Q2.18   If I change my employees' conditions do I have to issue new contracts?

Q2.19 If I forget to insert certain conditions into a contract what can I do to rectify the situation?

Q2.20 If I find that an employee gave me false or misleading information in his or her application can I dismiss that person?

Q2.21 What happens if an employer misrepresents a job?

Q2.22 I received a very adverse reference about a newly employed member of staff. What can I do?

Q2.23 What are the legal implications if, having entered into a contract with an employment agency for a permanent member of staff, the new recruit does not stay?

Q2.24 Can anyone else impose or imply terms into a contract?

3. PAY AND BENEFITS

Q3.1 What exactly is meant by "wages" in terms of the specific elements included?

Q3.2 What must I include in an itemised pay statement?

Q3.3 Am I obliged to provide holiday pay?

Q3.4 Do employees have the right to receive an advance on their wages when they join the organisation?

Q3.5 What rights have I got regarding the board and lodging I provide for my live-in staff?

Q3.6 How do I handle holiday pay and entitlement in a business which closes down in the winter months?

Q3.7 How do I recover overpayments of wages?

Q3.8 What deductions are authorised by the **Wages Act 1986**?

Q3.9 How can I get all my employees to be paid through a bank account?

Q3.10 How can I recover cash shortages after my employees have been incompetent in handling cash?

Q3.11 What remedies do employees have recourse to if they believe that unfair deductions have been made from their wages?

Q3.12 What happens regarding the payment of staff if the business fails?

Q3.13 Do I have to give equal pay to all employees when I have many different types of employees with varying lengths of service?

Q3.14 What elements of remuneration are counted when carrying out an analysis for equal pay purposes?

Q3.15   What arrangements must I make regarding the provision of pensions for my employees?

Q3.16   What regulations apply to personal gifts given by the employer to employees?

Q3.17   Are there any tax implications in respect of benefits and perks received by staff as part of their terms and conditions?

Q3.18   What is the current situation on National Insurance Contributions (NICs)?

Q3.19   How should I handle the payment of casual workers?

Q3.20   Should part-timers be paid on a pro-rata basis with full-time staff?

Q3.21   Do any regulations pertaining to Sunday trading affect the hospitality industry?

Q3.22   How should I deal with the administration of service charges and tipping?

Q3.23   What PAYE records must I maintain?

Q3.24   What is the present situation regarding minimum wages in the hospitality industry now that the Wages Councils have been abolished?

Q3.25   What legal obligations does an employer in the hospitality industry have to provide transport for female employees or to accompany them home when they finish work after 11.00pm?

Q3.26   Am I permitted to collect union dues from my employees' pay?

4. SICKNESS

Q4.1   Am I obliged to provide sick pay?

Q4.2   How do I handle Statutory Sick Pay (SSP) arrangements for new and existing employees?

Q4.3   What details should I give my staff about sickness schemes?

Q4.4   What action should I take in the case of an employee who has been absent through sickness on a long-term basis?

Q4.5   What are the guidelines for a self-certification procedure on sickness?

Q4.6   What measures can I take against an employee who regularly has a single day's absence from duty?

5. MATERNITY ISSUES

Q5.1   What time off for antenatal care must I give a pregnant employee?

Q5.2   What is the situation if an employee who only works two or three days a week asks for one or more of these days off for antenatal care?

Q5.3   What is the current situation regarding maternity leave?

Q5.4   Is an employee entitled to return to work after maternity leave?

Q5.5   Does an employee on maternity leave continue to have full use of all benefits, including a company car?

Q5.6   What is the difference between Statutory Maternity Pay (SMP) and the Maternity Allowance (MA)?

Q5.7   What records must I maintain regarding maternity pay?

Q5.8   Who pays Statutory Maternity Pay (SMP)?

6. HEALTH AND SAFETY AT WORK

Q6.1   As an employer, what are my responsibilities under common law for health and safety matters?

Q6.2   Who is affected by the **Health and Safety at Work Act 1974**, particularly regarding the issue of personal responsibility?

Q6.3   What key points should I communicate to employees about the **Health and Safety at Work Act 1974**?

Q6.4   How is the **Health and Safety at Work Act 1974** enforced?

Q6.5   What are the implications for my business of the recent **Management of Health and Safety Regulations 1992**?

Q6.6   What health and safety regulations affect me as an employer with regard to the working environment?

Q6.7   As a contract caterer, how am I affected by the 1992 Regulations on health and safety?

Q6.8   What exactly is repetitive strain injury (RSI)?

Q6.9   Should I be concerned about recent legislation on the reporting of dangerous occurrences and the control of dangerous substances?

Q6.10   What level of first aid cover must I provide, and does it apply to guests as well?

Q6.11   What are the proper procedures when dealing with infectious diseases?

Q6.12   What procedures can I introduce to insist that all employees have medical checks and are tested for HIV?

Q6.13   How am I affected by occupiers' liability?

Q6.14   Can an employer be liable for an employee's stress level?

Q6.15   I am considering introducing a policy regarding smoking at work. What should I be aware of?

7. HARASSMENT

Q7.1   When does a remark or act by one employee to another become a case of sexual harassment?

Q7.2   When does a remark or act by one employee to another become a case of sexual harassment, for example at a Christmas party off the premises?

Q7.3   To what extent is it the employer's responsibility to prevent or control an individual employee's behaviour if it is discriminatory?

Q7.4   How should a complaint from an employee that a colleague is "calling them names" be dealt with?

8. RECORDS, REFERENCES AND DATA PROTECTION

Q8.1   Does the law specify any records that I am obliged to keep regarding my employees?

Q8.2   What restrictions are placed on the information I keep concerning my employees?

Q8.3   What rights do my employees have to see the information I keep about them?

Q8.4   What data would you advise me to keep to ensure that I do not fall foul of equal opportunities law?

Q8.5   Am I obliged to give a reference concerning an ex-employee or one about to leave my employment?

Q8.6   Can an ex-employee bring an action against me as a result of a reference I have written?

Q8.7   Can employees see references I have received about them, or can past employees ask for details of references I have written about them?

Q8.8   Am I responsible to another employer as result of a reference I provide for him or her concerning an ex-employee of mine?

9. EMPLOYEE RELATIONS

Q9.1   Am I obliged to have a means of consulting with staff on any matters concerning their employment?

Q9.2   We have a trade union in our organisation which represents a number of our employees. What information do I have to pass on to this trade union?

Q9.3   Am I obliged to recognise and negotiate with a trade union which claims to have a significant number of my employees as members?

Q9.4   Can I refuse to employ someone because of his or her membership of a trade union?

Q9.5   Can I refuse to employ someone because of his or her refusal to join a trade union?

Q9.6   What rights to time off do union members have?

Q9.7   Can I dismiss someone because they took part in trade union activities at a time inconvenient to the business?

Q9.8   Can I dismiss someone because they took part in industrial action, eg a strike?

Q9.9   Can a trade union be sued for damages for inducing breaches of employment contracts?

Q9.10   Does the "closed shop" still exist?

Q9.11   As an employer, am I obliged to help a union to conduct a ballot on our premises?

10. TRANSFER OF UNDERTAKINGS

Q10.1   What is meant by a "transfer of undertakings"?

Q10.2   Are public sector organisations covered by the **Transfer of Undertakings (Protection of Employment) Regulations 1981**?

Q10.3   What is the link between transfer of undertakings regulations and the Acquired Rights Directive?

Q10.4   If a catering contract changes hands, do the staff all have to be made redundant or could some be transferred?

Q10.5   By law, what information regarding my employees' pay and benefits do I have to provide to a prospective purchaser or contractor of the undertaking?

Q10.6   If I acquire staff, do I become liable for accrued benefits, etc?

Q10.7   Can an incoming contractor offer terms and conditions of service that are less favourable to the employees?

Q10.8   If not all relevant information was disclosed to me when I took over a contract, what action can I take?

Q10.9   If an employee is dismissed as a result of a transfer, can that employee claim compensation for unfair dismissal?

Q10.10 If employees who transfer are members of a recognised trade union, is that recognition also transferred?

11. REDUNDANCY

Q11.1 What is redundancy?

Q11.2 What general guidance is there on the selection of employees for redundancy?

Q11.3 Can I simply keep my better employees when deciding on redundancies?

Q11.4 What is a claim of unfair selection for redundancy?

Q11.5 How are redundancy payments calculated?

Q11.6 How do I calculate continuous employment?

Q11.7 What is the basis of the calculation of an average weekly wage?

Q11.8 Can part-time workers receive redundancy payments?

Q11.9 Would an employee currently on maternity leave qualify for a redundancy payment?

Q11.10 What are my obligations concerning consultation with the workforce regarding redundancy?

Q11.11 Do I have to offer alternative employment to a redundant employee if it is available?

Q11.12 Can an employee refuse to accept alternative employment, and would this affect his or her rights to a redundancy payment?

Q11.13 Do I have to give employees who may be made redundant time off for job seeking and training?

Q11.14 What can be done to minimise the impact of redundancy on employees?

Q11.15 How long can employees "try out" a new job within the company without losing their rights to redundancy pay?

12. DISCIPLINE

Q12.1 What are my legal obligations regarding the disciplining and dismissal of employees?

Q12.2 What must I do to ensure that employees are aware of company rules, etc?

Q12.3 If employees are not performing satisfactorily, what must I do to improve the situation before taking disciplinary action?

Q12.4 Do employees have a right of representation during disciplinary procedures?

Q12.5 In what circumstances might it be appropriate to suspend an employee?

Q12.6 How long can a warning stay in place?

Q12.7   If I have a disciplinary procedure, do I have to follow it even for very serious cases of misconduct?

Q12.8   If two employees are known to be involved in a personal relationship, what rights does an employer have concerning this situation?

Q12.9   Do I need to use the disciplinary procedures with a new employee or can I simply terminate the employment?

13. DISMISSAL

Q13.1   What are the "fair" reasons for dismissal?

Q13.2   What is the difference between "wrongful" and "unfair" dismissal?

Q13.3   Which employees are protected against unfair dismissal?

Q13.4   What is the basis for the calculation of compensation in a case of unfair dismissal?

Q13.5   What is meant by constructive dismissal?

Q13.6   If an employee has been guilty of misconduct for some time, am I allowed to dismiss the employee?

Q13.7   Can I withhold pay for employees found guilty of misconduct?

Q13.8   Can I dismiss someone because of their behaviour outside the workplace?

Q13.9   Can I dismiss any employee for persistent, genuine illness?

Q13.10   What is the difference between dismissal and summary dismissal?

Q13.11   In what types of case will dismissal be automatically unlawful?

Q13.12   If I dismiss an employee for theft at work, and he or she is subsequently found not guilty in a criminal court, do I have to take the employee back?

14. TERMINATING CONTRACTS

Q14.1   How can I terminate a contract of employment?

Q14.2   Can I restrict who my employees work for after they leave my employment?

Q14.3   Can an employee resign without giving notice?

Q14.4   Can I dismiss staff without notice?

Q14.5   Can an employer withdraw notice once it has been given?

Q14.6   Can an employee withdraw his or her notice once it has been given?

Q14.7   Can a contract be terminated by events outside the control of the two parties to the contract?

15. INDUSTRIAL TRIBUNALS

Q15.1   What is the scope of cases covered by an industrial tribunal?

Q15.2   I have been called to attend an industrial tribunal as a result of a claim from a former employee. What processes are involved in this?

Q15.3   What remedies can an industrial tribunal take if an employee's claim is proven?

Q15.4   Can any general contractual matters be brought before a tribunal or would some matters go to a county court?

Q15.5   If an employee pursues a case in a tribunal, what documentation might the employer need, and would any official documentation be required?

Q15.6   Is it possible to settle claims without the case going to tribunal?

Q15.7   Do I need a lawyer to act on my behalf in a tribunal?

Q15.8   Is it possible to appeal against tribunal decisions?

1. RECRUITMENT

Q1.1 **What are the advantages of requiring job candidates to complete an application form?**

A. The main advantage is that all the information you require is set out in a standard format in the order that you have chosen. It also contains information you may wish to elicit fairly from all candidates that may not appear in full on an applicant's CV, eg driving licence information, why they think they are suitable for the job, etc.

If handwriting and accuracy are relevant criteria for a job, an application form may provide an employer with a first impression of neatness. Completing an application form requires more time than simply submitting a CV and may sift out a few candidates who are less committed to the job advertised. It enables an employer to compare like with like and in this way can be less discriminatory.

Q1.2 **Is the application form a legally binding document?**

A. Usually an application form asks the applicant to sign and verify that all the information disclosed is true. This being the case, contract law, including the **Misrepresentation Act 1967**, can be applied.

Q1.3 **When designing the application form may I ask questions about the number and ages of dependants the applicant may have?**

A. There is no law in the UK to stop an organisation presenting questions concerning family dependants in an application form, or indeed at an interview. However, an employer should be able to justify why the question is being asked, and ensure that all applicants are asked the same question. If an unsuccessful applicant lodged a claim of sex discrimination against an employer who had this information, the onus would be upon the employer to prove that no discrimination had taken place and that there had been another objectively justifiable reason for not offering this applicant the position available. The more important question would be "Is this person able to take on the full responsibilities of the job?" Attendance would be one of those responsibilities.

It is certainly not acceptable and would be contravening the **Sex Discrimination Act 1975** (direct discrimination) if an employer did not offer a female applicant a position because it was assumed that she would not be able to attend work at certain times.

Q1.4   Am I allowed to ask for a photograph?

A.   There is no law preventing you asking for a photograph. However, good practice would be to ask yourself whether a photograph is really essential. If a discrimination claim was made on the grounds of sex or race following an application for a post, it may not help the employer's case if a photograph had been requested. If an employer's argument is that appearance is important then it would be wise to ensure that such a factor appears clearly and unambiguously in a personnel specification.

Q1.5   What records must I keep for the selection of a candidate?

A.   There are no legal requirements to keep any specific records. However, it is good practice and advisable to keep records of the following for each job selection process:

- personnel specification (which describes the personal characteristics and qualifications needed)

- job description (which describes the job to be done)

- total number of applicants by ethnic group/sex

- those interviewed

- standard questions asked

- objective criteria for those turned down (preferably a standard format of assessment as provided in *Croner's Catering Records and Procedures*).

These should provide what would be necessary if a claim of discrimination is made against a prospective employer.

Q1.6 **At what point in the recruitment process may I apply for references?**

A. This will depend upon procedures and preferences of each organisation. Many public sector organisations apply for references prior to the interview (or other means of selection). Most other organisations appear to apply following the interview, and may even apply after the person has commenced employment. Whatever the choice, it is essential to ensure that the applicant's permission is sought first. This may appear on the application form, may be requested at the interview, or the offer of employment may be made subject to satisfactory references being received.

Q1.7 **Is there any limitation on the questions I can ask in a reference application?**

A. Strictly speaking there is no such limitation. However, any employer seeking a reference (as well as providing one) must bear in mind that the person giving the reference is legally responsible or liable if he or she makes untrue allegations which may harm another person's reputation.

As far back as 1936 (*Sim v Stretch* (1936) 52 TLR 669), defamation of character has been defined as "the publication of a statement about a person which reflects on a person's reputation". This includes in writing, on film or video, by word of mouth, gestures or sounds.

More recently, the House of Lords held that an employer is under a "duty of care" to a former employee when providing a reference (*Spring v Guardian Assurance plc* (1994) IRLR 460 — see *Caterer's Briefing* No. 41). A prospective employer may find it useful to receive tangible, factual information relating to the employee's attendance and punctuality, etc but more subjective information concerning attitudes may depend on the motivation of the employee, the job he or she was doing and who he or she worked with.

Q1.8   If an employee has been convicted of a criminal offence in the past, what rights do I have as an employer to have access to this information?

A.   An employee or prospective employee has the right to conceal details relating to what is called a "spent" conviction. Therefore, once a conviction is spent that person is not required by law to answer any questions concerning his or her past that cannot be answered without acknowledging or referring to the spent conviction. Failure to disclose a spent conviction cannot be used as grounds for dismissal or discrimination in any way. Gaps in a candidate's employment history may be explored but without any intention to discriminate on the grounds of spent conviction. Any other person who knows about the conviction (including an employer or previous employer) is also protected for failing to disclose the information.

The periods of time after which a conviction is spent vary according to the seriousness of the offence: some convictions are never spent. Some professionals are excluded from this protection and they always have to disclose previous convictions; these include accountants, solicitors, nurses and doctors.

Q1.9   Are there any legal obligations to advertise internally and externally for vacancies that occur?

A.   There is no law concerning whether or where an organisation may advertise for new recruits. Within the public sector (local government, civil service) it is frequently the policy that all positions must be advertised externally even if it is evident that a suitable candidate exists within the organisation. This practice, which has the advantage of drawing from a greater pool of new knowledge, skills and ideas, needs to be weighed against the effect of offering promotion or transfer opportunities to the existing workforce.

Q1.10 **More than 50% of the workforce in my organisation is female but there is only one female manager out of six. Are we breaking the law?**

A. There is no legal quota for the employment of men or women, although there have been voluntary initiatives to encourage the recruitment and promotion of women in the workplace, particularly at managerial level.

Under the **Sex Discrimination Act 1975** it is unlawful to discriminate on the grounds of sex or marital status. The Act covers discrimination in recruitment and selection, as well as during employment and in termination.

Direct discrimination is where a person is or would be treated less favourably than someone of the opposite sex.

Indirect discrimination is where an employer applies a requirement or condition which is such that the proportion of women that can comply is considerably smaller than the proportion of men able to, is not justifiable, and is to the woman's detriment because she cannot comply. This applies equally to men compared to women, although the number of cases of sex discrimination towards men still remains relatively low.

If the situation outlined in the question has arisen as a result of natural wastage or because of historical recruitment practices, you would need to ensure that when next recruiting, the opportunity was made open to both sexes.

Q1.11 **Are there any circumstances under which I can specify that I want to employ a man or a woman?**

A. The **Sex Discrimination Act 1975** outlines a number of instances where being a particular sex is a genuine occupational qualification (GOQ) for the job.

1. Where a particular physiology is required, (as opposed to physical stamina), eg if dramatic performance, entertainment or authenticity requires it.

2.   For reasons of decency or privacy; if the job involves close physical contact or state of undress with other employees, customers or persons, eg care home staff.

3.   Where the welfare or education of individuals is being provided and the recipients could identify better with a member of their own sex.

4.   Where the job is being carried out at a single sex institution, eg an all-female health club or a gentleman's club.

5.   Where accommodation is provided with the job, eg if there are limited bathroom facilities an employer may choose to retain the accommodation within one house as single sex and this may in turn limit the employer in who he or she recruits. However, it is only likely to be considered reasonable if the policy is consistent over a period of time.

6.   Where the work requires a married couple. It is legal for an employer to state that he or she requires or prefers a legally married couple. This has been particularly common in the past for pub management. In practice it is becoming less common.

7.   If the work is being undertaken outside the UK and the local laws and customs of that country may prohibit a particular sex from carrying out that work.

Q1.12   **During interviews I need to ascertain the candidates' ability to attend work without having too many domestic problems such as responsibilities for children. How can I find out what I need to know without being discriminatory?**

A.   As long as the same information is asked of all applicants regardless of sex, an employer may be seen to be fair. There is often a general assumption among employers in this country that it is the woman's responsibility to look after the children if required. In practice it is becoming more common that men may be single parents, or are taking joint responsibility for the family. It is unlawful to assume that a man is the breadwinner of a family (*Coleman v Skyrail Oceanic Ltd* (1981) IRLR 398) or that the woman is responsible for the child care (see answer to Q1.3).

Q1.13   What does indirect discrimination mean as far as race or nationality is concerned?

A.   The **Race Relations Act 1976** defines indirect discrimination in the same way as the **Sex Discrimination Act 1975** (see Q.1.10). Indirect discrimination occurs if a condition of employment means that the proportion of persons from a particular racial group able to meet the condition is considerably smaller than the proportion not of that racial group. If a condition is justifiable irrespective of a racial group then there is no discrimination. The onus is on the employer to prove that the condition is objectively justified.

Q1.14   Are there any circumstances under which I can specify that I want to employ a particular nationality or race?

A.   The **Race Relations Act 1976** outlines a number of genuine occupational qualifications (GOQs) where it is legal to specify a particular nationality or race. These are:

– for entertainment and dramatic performances

– artists or photographic models

– personal services for the welfare of a particular ethnic group, eg health visitor

– authenticity, eg Asian waiting staff in an Asian restaurant.

The last point is the most likely to occur within the catering industry. It should be noted that a Chinese chef for a Chinese restaurant would be unlikely to fall into this category unless there was an open-plan kitchen visible to the customers and therefore forming part of the atmosphere.

Q1.15 **Can I legally discriminate against a person whose religious activities require him or her to attend certain services and festivals, etc which conflict with work requirements?**

A.   The **Race Relations Act 1976** prohibits discrimination against a person on the grounds of colour, race, nationality or ethnic or national origins.

An ethnic group is defined as having two main characteristics:

– a long shared history

– a cultural tradition of its own, often, but not necessarily, associated with religious observance.

Other relevant characteristics include:

– a common ancestry

– a common language

– a common literature

– a common religion

– being a minority, oppressed or dominant group.

Q1.16 **Is there a minimum size of organisation below which sex and race discrimination legislation does not apply?**

A.   No, it applies to all organisations dealing with job applicants, employees, contracted workers, partners and any self-employed persons who may be working for an organisation.

Q1.17 **Are there any discriminatory implications of using psychometric tests as part of the selection process?**

A.   There has been considerable concern over the fairness of selection and assessment testing in relation to equal opportunities. What has been revealed is that whilst properly constructed tests have been found to predict the likelihood of succeeding in a job better than any other measure, they may not truly reflect the abilities of ethnic minority groups, or may contain a gender bias towards males. For example, a verbal reasoning test used by

British Rail for driver applicants was found to have a disadvantageous effect on those who spoke English as their second language.

Saville & Holdsworth Ltd has published a set of guidelines in conjunction with the Commission for Race Relations and the Equal Opportunities Commission, called *Equal Opportunities Guidelines for Best Test Practice in the Use of Personnel Selection Tests.*

Q1.18 **We have a predominantly young workforce. Am I legally permitted to stipulate an age limit when recruiting employees?**

A. At the time of going to print, no legislation exists in the UK to prevent employers from discriminating on the basis of age when they recruit staff. So far the Government has rejected calls for legislation to prevent age discrimination. The current demographic trends (a quarter of the population is over 55 years of age and 2 million of the 3 million plus unemployed are over the age of 45) are to continue into the next decade. Some other countries have introduced age discrimination laws, including the USA, Canada, France and some Australian states. In 1990, the Institute of Personnel Management (now the Institute of Personnel and Development) published a set of guidelines to encourage professional personnel managers to consider older applicants when filling vacancies. It is therefore very likely that the issue of legislation will be addressed in the near future.

Q1.19 **What are my obligations regarding the employment of disabled persons?**

A. The **Disability Discrimination Act 1995** recently superseded the **Disabled Persons (Employment) Act 1944** and **1958**. The Act makes it unlawful to discriminate against a disabled person in the selection process, in the terms upon which a job is offered to a disabled person, in the opportunities offered for promotion, training, transfer or any other benefit, or in dismissing a disabled person.

The Act also contains a duty on employers to make adjustments, either in arrangements made (such as finding a ground floor office for a wheelchair-bound employee if a building has no lift) or in any physical feature of the premises (such as providing an access ramp or doorways wide enough for wheelchairs). Toilet facilities sufficiently spacious to accommodate a wheelchair would also fit into this category.

The legislation covers employers of more than 20 staff. It repeals the previous quota system and the requirement to ensure that 3% of the workforce are disabled.

Q1.20 **What restrictions are there for the employment of persons under the age of 18 within the catering industry?**

A. The employment of young persons, ie those under 18 but over school leaving age, used to be controlled by a number of statutes. The sections of these Acts relating to hours, holidays, restrictions on young men working underground, the need to keep registers and the power to require medical supervision were all repealed by the **Employment Act 1989**. As far as the employment of children (16 or under) is concerned, no child may be employed:

– who is under the age of 13

– during school hours

– before 07.00 and after 19.00

– for more than two hours during any school day

– for more than two hours on a Sunday

– to lift, carry or move anything so heavy as to be likely to cause injury to himself or herself.

It is advisable to contact the local careers office or Jobcentre for details of any by-laws that may exist which further restrict the employment of those under the age of 16.

Licensing legislation provides that those under 18 cannot work in a bar (ie where the sale and consumption of alcohol takes place) but they may work in licensed premises which are not a bar, eg in a licensed restaurant. Specific advice should be sought from a local legal advisor or the police before employing young people in licensed premises.

Q1.21 **What permits are required for potential employees from within and outside the European Union (EU)?**

A. The employment of EU nationals does not require the authorisation of the Department for Education and Employment. The right to free movement is embodied in Article 48 of the Treaty of Rome. Non-EU nationals who are subject to immigration control must have a work permit unless they fall into one of the limited permit-free categories, eg Commonwealth citizens who can prove that one grandparent was born in the UK. The prospective employer must obtain the permit for a specific job before the person enters the country by completing form WP1. A permit will not be granted if, in the opinion of the Department for Education and Employment, suitable resident labour is available to fill the post, or if the conditions of employment offered are less favourable than those offered in the area for similiar work. The scheme is therefore aimed at workers of degree level or who have specialist skills or qualifications. Permits are normally issued for a limited period of up to four years.

Non-EU students also need permission to work even if it is part of their course, but not if they are on a course in the UK.

2. CONTRACTS

Q2.1   **What are my general duties as an employer towards my employees?**

A.   Most of an employer's duties to his or her employees are defined by the employment contract or by statutes, most of which will be expanded upon throughout the course of this pocket book. However, several common law (law derived from custom or judicial precedent) obligations have been imposed upon employers over the years by judges' decisions. The consequences of being in breach of these common law obligations are that the employee, if suffering loss or injury, can sue for money compensation known as damages. Furthermore, he or she may have the right to resign without notice if the employer's breach of contract is sufficiently serious. The principal obligations on the employer are listed below.

1.   *The duty to pay.* Where no wages have been agreed, the courts may imply reasonable remuneration into the contract of employment.

2.   *The duty to provide work.* Generally speaking, so long as an employer pays his or her employee he or she is not obliged to provide work, ie he or she can lay off staff on full pay (or as agreed by contract). The general principle on the implied duty to provide work was stated in *Collier v Sunday Referee Publishing Co. Ltd* (1940) 2 KB 647.

In some cases there is an obligation to provide work, particularly where the amount to be earned by the employee is determined by the amount of work done. Other situations might arise when the employee needs to work to enhance his or her reputation (such as an actor playing a leading role) or where damage could be done to a person's professional reputation should it become known that he or she was not working.

3. *Health and safety.* Whilst most health and safety issues are now covered by statute and regulations, there are still common law contractual duties placed upon an employer concerning employees' health and safety. This duty is considered to contain three basic elements:

   – to select reasonably competent employees

   – to provide adequate materials

   – to provide a safe system of working.

   If the employer is in breach of any of the above and the employee suffers either physical or mental injury as a result, the employee could sue the employer for damages and/or resign. The employer could also be prosecuted under health and safety legislation.

4. *The duty to behave reasonably.* There is a duty on both parties to behave reasonably and to do nothing that would undermine the mutual confidence that the two parties to the contract have in each other.

Q2.2 **What are the general duties owed by an employee to his or her employer?**

A.   Most duties will be defined by the contract itself or by statute. However, the courts have developed some general principles which are as follows.

1. *The duty to serve.* The employee has an obligation to serve the employer within the terms of the employment contract. The relationship between an employer and employee, under a contract of service, is a personal one, ie an employee cannot delegate to another person (although it is not uncommon in some situations — at the discretion of the employer — for employees to send members of their family or friends to cover for them). There is no obligation on the employee to be at the employer's disposal all the time — only within the terms of the contract.

2.   *The duty to be obedient.* An employee is under a duty to be obedient, but this does not mean that an employer can ask him or her to do absolutely anything. The employee must only obey all lawful orders that are within the terms of the employment contract.

3.   *Competence and duty of care.* With few exceptions (eg where training is to be provided), by entering into the employment contract an employee promises that he or she is competent to do the work involved. As a consequence, lack of competence may be a breach of contract which could lead to dismissal and even (in extreme circumstances) to an action for damages.

4.   *The duty of good faith.* The relationship between an employer and employee is one of good faith. This is divided into a number of different duties.

   • Secret profits. The employee must not accept secret profits or commissions. It is quite common in the catering industry, with employees responsible for purchasing supplies, for "backhanders" or gifts to be given. An employee is obliged to inform the employer of such gifts. Failure to do so could enable the employer to dismiss the employee for breach of contract.

   • Confidential information. Employees must not divulge confidential information about their employer's business or about their employer.

   • Inventions and copyright. Copyright and patents acquired in the course of employment are normally the property of the employer, although some employment contracts provide for these to remain the property of the employee (**Copyright Act 1956** and **Patent Act 1977**).

   • Disclosure of breach of duty. Employees, particularly those in positions of responsibility, may be under a duty to disclose to the employer any breaches of duty by other employees.

Q2.3 **How can I distinguish between an employee and a subcontractor such as a gardener, a window cleaner or even a home worker who works for me?**

A. It is not always easy to determine if a worker is an employee or a subcontractor. The distinction, however, is vital because in the case of subcontractors they are responsible for their own tax affairs, whereas in the case of employees the employer is responsible. Should the Inland Revenue decide that a subcontractor is in fact an employee, the back tax is the liability of the employer. The main difference is that an employee is a party to a contract *of* service whereas in the case of a subcontract the two parties are parties to a contract *for* services.

Section 153(1) of the **Employment Protection (Consolidation) Act 1978** defines an employee as "an individual who has entered into or works under a contract of employment". A contract of employment is also defined as a contract of service. However, to determine if someone is really an employee in law, a number of tests have been developed by the courts.

1. *The control test.* In general, this tests the extent to which the employer "has control" over the worker in question. A worker works sufficiently under the control of an employer to qualify as an employee if the employer not only instructs the worker what to do, but also how and when to do it. Clearly, employees such as waiting staff or bar staff would fall under the definition of employee when the control test is applied. The answer is much less clear when the test is applied, for example, to a gardener, a window cleaner or a musician, who may all work for several other people.

2. *The business integration test.* To what extent is the worker and his or her work an integral part of the business? A cook

working for a restaurant is central to the business, whereas a window cleaner's or a musician's work is ancillary to it (*Stevenson Jordan and Harrison Ltd v Macdonald and Evans* (1952) 1 TLR 108). In contrast, a musician working for an orchestra may well be deemed an employee because the business of the orchestra is music (*Whittaker v Minister for Pensions and National Insurance* (1966) 3 All ER 531).

3. *The multiple test.* The multiple test adopts a broad approach and would expect that:

    (a) the worker agrees to provide his or her own work and skill to the employer in return for a wage or other remuneration

    (b) he or she will be subject to the other's control

    (c) the other provisions of the contract are consistent with it being a contract of service *(Ready-Mixed Concrete (South East) Ltd v Minister of Pensions and National Insurance* (1968) 1 All ER 433).

In the case of home workers, eg someone who regularly cooks food in his or her own home for transfer to a restaurant or pub, it is important to establish if the relationship is an employment relationship. For there to be an employment relationship there should be some form of obligation on both sides, ie to give and to accept work. This does not exist in a straightforward sale of goods — neither side is obliged to sell or to buy. However, if there was a well-founded expectation because there was a regular giving and taking of work over a period of years, an employment relationship may exist. Recently the Court of Appeal confirmed that there is no "all purpose" test for employment status — all relevant circumstances have to be taken into account (*Hall (Inspector of Taxes) v Lorimer* (1994) IRLR 171).

Q2.4   **If I employ staff from an agency are they employees of our organisation?**

A.   This may depend upon frequency of work and length of service. It may be deemed that the organisation is the "principal" employer and has an employment relationship with the employee. If this is the case then some legislation such as the **Employment Protection (Consolidation) Act 1978** applies. If the staff are seen to be contracted workers from another employer some legislation such as the **Health and Safety at Work Act 1974** still applies.

Q2.5   **How can I distinguish between a full-time employee and a part-time employee?**

A.   Until recently many employers distinguished, in practice, between full-time and part-time employees mainly through the number of hours worked and through offering different conditions. Today, no contractual distinction is necessary because the law treats full-time and part-time employees the same. Indeed, to differentiate on terms and conditions between the two could lead to a successful sex discrimination case, since more women than men are part-time workers.

As a rough guideline, full-time employees tend to work around 30–45 hours over five days, for about 48 weeks a year. Part-time employees may work for as little as one session a week involving only three or four hours. Both full-time and part-time employees now benefit, pro-rata (where relevant), from similar conditions such as the right to written particulars and itemised pay statements, minimum statutory notice, time off for public and trade union duties, maternity leave, holiday entitlements and pay, sick pay and pension schemes (**Employment Protection (Part-time Employees) Regulations 1995** (SI 1995 No. 31)). See Table 1 on page 19 for a list of rights in employment.

Q2.6   How can I distinguish between a part-time employee and a casual worker?

A.   In essence, a casual worker is one who works on a contract for a limited period such as one evening session in a bar, or for 10 days for a special occasion such as a hotel Christmas programme. This is to be distinguished from workers who have agreed to work regularly, for example every Saturday evening. In the definitive case (*O'Kelly and others v Trusthouse Forte plc* (1983) IRLR 369), the Court of Appeal ruled that casuals were not employees because:

- the engagement was terminable without notice

- the worker had the right to accept or to refuse the work

- the company was not obliged to provide work.

Q2.7   Is it important to be able to make distinctions between types of employee?

A.   It is extremely important to distinguish between casual workers and regular workers. Workers employed on regular contracts, as opposed to casual contracts, have a range of rights which an employer is obliged to meet. These are shown in the table below. Casual workers, even those who work regularly for an employer (but on session by session contracts) have no such rights. In the case of casual workers, an employer's commitments end (apart from income tax and National Insurance obligations) at the end of the work session concerned. In the case of regular workers this is not the case.

It is good practice to issue casual employees, when they are first employed, with a letter explaining their employment status.

Table 1: Qualifying Continuous Service for Employees' Rights

Right	Minimum Service
Protection from discrimination on grounds of race or sex	None
Statement of terms and conditions of employment	1 month*
Pay during medical suspension	1 month
Guarantee payments	1 month
Right to union membership and to take part in union activities	None
Time off work for: union duties	None
union activities	None
safety representatives	None
public duties	None
redundant employees	2 years
antenatal care	None
Statutory Maternity Pay (SMP): lower rate	26 weeks
higher rate	26 weeks
Right to return to work after maternity absence	2 years†
Right to basic maternity leave	None
Itemised pay statement	None
Written reasons for dismissal	2 years
Minimum notice of termination of employment	1 month
Right not to be unfairly dismissed	2 years
Redundancy pay	2 years

Notes

* The statement must be issued within 2 months of the start of employment.

† Unless the organisation has fewer than 5 employees.

Q2.8   What constitutes a contract of employment?

A.   Many employers and managers do not distinguish between what is known as the "statement of main terms and conditions of employment" as required by the **Employment Protection (Consolidation) Act 1978** (EP(C)A) and what is, in effect, the common law contract.

The common law contract is much wider-ranging than the written statement required by the EP(C)A. The common law contract consists of the offer made by the employer which may include a range of terms and conditions, possibly deriving from the original advertisement, statements made at interview and at induction, company documents such as house rules, job descriptions and trade practices, etc. In addition, the contract may have been modified over time by new conditions being agreed by both parties. It may also incorporate terms and conditions agreed with a recognised trade union.

The written statement required by the EP(C)A has to be given to employees within two months of starting employment (see Q2.11).

It is good practice, however, to issue a full contract of employment (incorporating everything required by the EP(C)A and all other important conditions) before an employee starts employment. The employee should be asked to sign and return a copy as acceptance of the position.

Q2.9   Do contracts of employment have to be in writing?

A.   The common law of contract does not require contracts, including employment contracts, to be in writing. Indeed many employment contracts, particularly part-time and casual contracts, are not in writing, often having been agreed over the telephone.

However, the **Employment Protection (Consolidation) Act 1978**, as stated above, does require all regular employees who have worked for at least one month to receive a written statement within two months of employment starting.

Q2.10 **Does the written statement of terms and conditions as required by the Employment Protection (Consolidation) Act 1978 constitute a contract of employment for legal purposes?**

A.   No, because the written statement of terms and conditions as required by the **Employment Protection (Consolidation) Act 1978** only requires certain conditions to be in writing — the total contract of employment may be much more comprehensive (see Q2.8 above).

Q2.11 **When does the written statement of terms and conditions, as required by the Employment Protection (Consolidation) Act 1978, have to be given to an employee?**

A.   This has to be given to all employees (other than casual workers) who have worked for one month, within two months of starting employment (see Table 1 on page 19).

A written statement does not have to be given to an employee if:

– the employment lasts for less than one month

– the employee is employed mainly outside the UK

– the employee is a seaman.

Q2.12 **Am I free to negotiate any conditions into a contract?**

A.   Under contract law, the offeror (the person making the contract) is normally allowed to incorporate any conditions he or she wishes — it is up to the offeree (the person receiving the offer) to decide whether to accept these conditions.

However, there are certain terms which, if included in contracts, may be void in law. Many contracts with restrictive covenants, eg restrictions on the future employment of existing employees (eg not to compete) have been held to be void (*Cantor Fitzgerald (UK) Ltd v Wallace* (1992) IRLR 215).

It is not possible to insert clauses into a contract which remove or reduce an employee's statutory or common law rights, eg length of notice or health and safety rights, except in exceptional circumstances.

Q2.13 **How specific can I be in applying standards required for dress code, wearing jewellery and appearance, etc?**

A. There have been a number of cases concerning hair length, the wearing of earrings and the application of a dress code in the last few years.

In *Smith v Safeway plc* (1995) IRLR 132 EAT, a delicatessen assistant was dismissed because his ponytail had grown too long to fit under his hat. Company rules required men's hair to be above their shirt collars; women could have shoulder-length hair provided it was tied back. Mr Smith claimed this amounted to direct discrimination in breach of s.1(1)(a) of the **Sex Discrimination Act 1975**. His claim was upheld by the Employment Appeal Tribunal (EAT), which took the view that the employee's treatment had been less favourable than that of women and that the employer's requirements could be applied equally to both sexes without restricting men's hair length. However, it may not be appropriate to transfer this judgment to all catering workers. Each case will be judged on its particular circumstances.

A previous case concerning a woman who wished to wear trousers in the bookshop where she was employed (*Schmidt v Austicks Bookshops Ltd* (1977) IRLR 360) was not upheld, on the basis that the EAT considered that rules about dress may be applied even if those rules may be different for males and females. In this case, female employees were permitted to wear trousers only in the stockroom and not where they could be seen by customers. The EAT ruled that no comparable provision could be applied to male employees. There has been a more recent case concerning a transvestite taxi driver who claimed that his employer had discriminated against him for not allowing him to wear a skirt to work. He lost the case as it was deemed to be "inappropriate" in a business environment. In *Smith v Safeway*, the final view (although divided) was that a restriction on hair length affected a person at all times unlike other rules on appearance (eg the wearing of certain clothes applies during working hours only).

Rules may be set out that are considered reasonable for the type of operation of the business with, for example, due consideration of a "conventional" image, if required. In general, tribunals accept that certain styles may be unacceptable to most customers in certain types of businesses. However, particular care should be taken to avoid any discriminatory aspects when setting standards on the wearing of rings, earrings and hair length and the same appearance codes should be adopted for both sexes as far as possible. Public perception of acceptability is constantly changing and employers need to regularly review their rules.

In addition to ensuring that dress codes are not discriminatory on the grounds of sex, employers also need to be aware of religious requirements. For example, Sikhs have special dispensation to allow them to wear a turban instead of a safety helmet (**Employment Act 1989**, s.11). A ban on beards would exclude all orthodox Sikhs (although it may be acceptable on the grounds of hygiene) and a ban on dreadlocks would exclude certain Afro-Caribbean religious sects. All employees' dress/appearance must meet the requirements of the **Food Safety Act 1990**.

Q2.14   What has to be specified in a contract?

A.   The **Employment Protection (Consolidation) Act 1978** specifies that the following items have to be included in the written statement:

(a)   the names of the employer and employee

(b) the date when employment began

(c) the date on which the employee's period of continuous employment began (taking into account any employment with a previous employer which counts)

(d) the scale or rate of pay, or the way pay is worked out

(e) the pay intervals (hourly, weekly or monthly, etc)

(f) any terms and conditions relating to hours of work (including normal working hours)

(g) any terms and conditions relating to holiday entitlement including public holidays and holiday pay (including rules on entitlement to accrued holiday pay on termination of employment) — these rules must be sufficiently specific to allow the entitlement to be precisely calculated

(h) job title or a brief job description

(i) place of work or, if the employee is required or permitted to work at various places, an indication of that fact and the employer's address.

The employer must also provide the following within the two month period (either in further instalments or with the principal statement):

(a) any terms and conditions relating to sickness or injury, including sick pay

(b) rules on pension and pension schemes (this requirement does not apply where the employee's pension rights derive from a statutory scheme under which the employer is already required to provide such information)

(c) length of notice to be given by both employer and employee

(d) if the contract is temporary, an indication of the expected duration, or the end date of a fixed-term contract

(e) particulars of any collective agreements which directly affect the terms and conditions of the employment including, where the employer is not a party, the persons by whom they were made

(f)   where the employee is required to work outside the UK for a period of more than one month: details of the length of posting, the currency in which payment will be made, details of any additional benefits arising from the posting, and any terms and conditions relating to the employee's return to the UK. If the employee is to begin work outside the UK within two months of starting, all the particulars must be given before the employee leaves.

The statement must also include the following details:

(a)   any disciplinary rules applicable

(b)   the name (or job title) of the person to whom an employee can apply if dissatisfied with a disciplinary decision, and the manner in which such applications can be made

(c)   the name (or job title) of the person with whom the employee can raise a grievance and the manner in which such applications should be made

(d)   an explanation of any additional steps in the disciplinary or grievance procedures.

The ACAS Code of Practice on Discipline recommends that employers have clearly stated disciplinary rules which all employees know and that a person to whom an employee can appeal against a disciplinary decision is someone more senior than the person who made the decision.

An employer who has fewer than 20 employees (including those of associated employers) on the date an employee's continuous service began is not required to supply particulars of disciplinary rules or procedures to that employee (although the employer must still provide details of how to pursue a grievance).

Details of disciplinary or grievance procedures relating to health or safety at work do not have to be included.

Q2.15 Can other documents be incorporated into a contract?

A. Yes. It is quite in order to incorporate other documents into contracts. These can be house rules, operational manuals, company
induction booklets and pension rules, etc. However, these cannot
contain substantial conditions or changes to conditions that were
not communicated before employment started. It is also possible
to incorporate into the individual contract the terms of a collective
agreement with a trade union or staff association, etc.

**Q2.16 Does the law specify any minimum or maximum conditions in
employment contracts such as pay, hours of work, holidays
and sick pay, etc?**

A. Until relatively recently, minimum wages for the catering industry
and many other industries were set by Wages Councils. These no
longer exist, so there are no minimum conditions laid down by law.
There are, of course, Statutory Sick Pay and Statutory Maternity
Pay schemes, which are covered in chapters 4 and 5 respectively.

**Q2.17 How can I change the conditions of employment of my em-
ployees?**

A. Once a contract has been made it is, in principle, not possible to
modify it except by mutual consent. In fact, a new offer has to be
made and accepted by the employee. However, the courts have
upheld the right of employers to make minor unilateral changes to
contracts on the basis that the employees should agree to co-
operate and obey lawful orders and instructions. Any variation
made under a "unilateral variation" clause would have to be
reasonable in the circumstances. For example, unless a relocation
clause was also contained in the contract, it is unlikely that the
decision to transfer an employee from one country to another
under a unilateral variation clause would be upheld in court.

If an employer wishes to change a contract and the employee
refuses the proposed change, the employer can terminate the

contract within the terms of the contract and statute law and offer a new one on the required terms. If the employee does not wish to accept the new terms he or she could possibly claim unfair dismissal or constructive dismissal and also sue for breach of contract.

If a contract is terminated and a new one offered on different terms, it is vital that the termination and new offer are made clear (*Burdett-Coutts and others v Hertfordshire County Council* (1984) IRLR 91).

Q2.18 If I change my employees' conditions do I have to issue new contracts?

A.   Although under common law there is no requirement to make or alter contracts in writing, it is good business practice to confirm all contracts in writing so that there is less room for misunderstanding should any disagreement arise. However, under the **Employment Protection (Consolidation) Act 1978** an employer must give employees individual written notification of any changes to those conditions which come within the scope of the Act within one month of the change taking effect. Details of the change must be given in full, although the statement may refer the employee to other documents. Where an employer changes or the employer changes name, the employee must be notified in writing of the new name of the employer and the date when continuous employment began. (See chapter 10 on Transfer of Undertakings).

Q2.19 If I forget to insert certain conditions into a contract what can I do to rectify the situation?

A.   The answer to this question is basically the same as the answer to Q2.17. In essence, you have to make a new offer and obtain acceptance of this.

Q2.20 **If I find that an employee gave me false or misleading information in his or her application can I dismiss that person?**

A.   Under s.1 of the **Misrepresentation Act 1967**, "where a person enters into a contract after a misrepresentation, and that misrepresentation has become a term of the contract, or the contract has been formed, then he or she will be able to rescind the contract."

From this, it is apparent that if an applicant for a position claims a qualification or experience which he or she does not have, then the employer may have the right to rescind the contract. In practice, many employees will exaggerate their claims to skills or experience and so employers have to decide if the misrepresentation is fundamental or merely a "slight change of emphasis". For example, if an applicant for a head chef's position claimed to have controlled a brigade of 20 but had never actually controlled more than five, this could be deemed to be a misrepresentation.

Q2.21 **What happens if an employer misrepresents a job?**

A.   If an employer misrepresents a job, the employee can rescind the contract and could also sue for damages (*McNally v Welltrade International, T James and Welltrade Middle East Ltd* (1978) IRLR 497).

Q2.22 **I received a very adverse reference about a newly employed member of staff. What can I do?**

A.   Often an offer of employment is made subject to certain conditions, such as the achievement of a qualification or the receipt of satisfactory references. It is quite in order for an employer to make a conditional offer so long as the condition is made absolutely clear. If the condition is not complied with then there is no offer outstanding to be accepted.

If the employee has already started employment the same principle applies and as the employee has to be employed for two years to qualify for unfair dismissal protection, the employer might rescind the contract without fear of the employee taking the case to an industrial tribunal (unless the employee chooses to use reasons such as race, sex or trade union discrimination as a reason). However, the two year protection rule may be removed as a result of cases pending.

Q2.23 **What are the legal implications if, having entered into a contract with an employment agency for a permanent member of staff, the new recruit does not stay?**

A.   An employment agency should have a set of standard terms and conditions of business which it will present to a prospective client. In addition to this, it may encourage an employer to enter a specific customised contract with it that provides the employer with preferential commission rates, and the agency with a guaranteed "head start" as and when vacancies arise.

As with any contract entered into, the answer to this question will depend upon what has been agreed. This may be in the form of a contract or simply a letter of a more general nature, with the agreement being the general terms and conditions of business that the agency uses. Agencies may have a minimum introduction fee and usually charge a percentage of the salary being paid and this varies according to the level or job grade. They will usually include a scale of rebates if the employment is terminated within the first few weeks of employment. It is advisable to read the small print before entering into any agreement, and negotiate individual terms if desirable.

Q2.24 **Can anyone else impose or imply terms into a contract?**

A.   Where parties to a contract have not included a term or terms into a contract, a court may imply a term or terms (*Gardner Ltd v Beresford* (1978) IRLR 63).

An industrial tribunal may insert terms into the statement issued under the **Employment Protection (Consolidation) Act 1978.**

3. PAY AND BENEFITS

Q3.1 **What exactly is meant by "wages" in terms of the specific elements included?**

A. The **Wages Act 1986** modernised the law in terms of the payment of wages and salaries. Under the Act, "wages" is deemed to mean any sums payable to the employee by the employer in connection with that employment. It includes any fee, bonus, commission, holiday pay or other emolument relevant to the employment, whether specified in the contract of employment or not (*Kent Management Services Ltd v Butterfield* (1992) ICR 272). Wages also include statutory payments, such as Statutory Sick Pay (SSP), Statutory Maternity Pay (SMP), guarantee payments, payment for time off for union duties, payment for time off for antenatal care and payment while under medical suspension.

Wages do not include the repayment of expenses, any advance on wages, any compensation or severance pay or any redundancy pay. Payments in kind are normally excluded from the definition of wages except items like luncheon vouchers, which are transferable into a fixed monetary value. Payments in lieu of notice are not wages, as these are paid after the termination of the contract — in effect to compensate for breach of the contract to provide work (*Delaney v Staples* (1992) ICR 483). When compensation is considered at an industrial tribunal, a week's pay is taken as the gross pay under the contract, or the average of the last 12 weeks' pay if piece rate, regular overtime or commission applies (*Cooner v PS Doal & Son* (1988) IRLR 338 EAT).

Q3.2 **What must I include in an itemised pay statement?**

A. Under the **Employment Protection (Consolidation) Act 1978**, every employee must be given, on or before pay-day, an itemised pay statement, containing the following details:

- gross amount of wages
- net amount of wages
- variable deductions and the purposes for which they are made
- fixed deductions and the purposes for which they are made
- where different parts of the net amount are paid in different ways, the amount and method of payment for each part payment
- if a company operates an Inland Revenue approved profit-related pay scheme (PRP), the pay slip must show PRP separate from gross pay.

This requirement applies regardless of hours worked.

The statement of fixed deductions does not have to be given each time if, instead, employees have been given a standing statement of such fixed deductions. This standing statement must be updated every 12 months. The easier it is to understand the pay statement, the less confusion and fewer problems there are likely to be.

Q3.3   Am I obliged to provide holiday pay?

A.   Surprisingly, there is no legal requirement in the UK for an employer to provide paid annual leave. In practice, very few organisations make no provisions for paid holidays and the entitlement to holiday pay is a matter for the interpretation of the contractual obligation. There is no automatic entitlement for bank holidays, although it is customary in most cases. It is also the case that there is no legal right to be paid for accrued holidays which have not been taken by the end of the holiday year, provided the opportunity to take holiday entitlement was provided (*Morley v Heritage plc* (1993) IRLR 401).

Q3.4   Do employees have the right to receive an advance on their wages when they join the organisation?

A.   It will depend upon what has been stated in the contract, a personnel practices document or what may have occurred in the past (custom and practice). It is not uncommon for large employers to offer this facility for new recruits who are to be paid monthly.

Q3.5 **What rights have I got regarding the board and lodging I provide for my live-in staff?**

A. In the hotel business, the provision of live-in accommodation with all meals supplied is still a common occurrence, though it can lead to many disputes, for example concerning the maintenance of the facilities and the procedure when employment is terminated. The terms and conditions must be clearly set out. The accommodation is best provided on a licence which can be terminated upon termination of employment, for whatever reason that may be. The provisions of this arrangement should specify that the employee is responsible for maintaining the fixtures and fittings at the standard they were when the employee entered the accommodation, when a detailed inventory of contents and their condition should be undertaken. The penalties for damage should be spelt out in both disciplinary and financial terms. The arrangements for inspections of the room(s) should also be clear. Above all, it must be clear that when the employee leaves his or her employment, on the effective date of termination, he or she must vacate the premises.

The termination of an employee's licence to occupy residential accommodation provided by the employer does not have to comply with the notice provisions of the **Protection from Eviction Act 1977.**

On the financial side, note that the provision of free board and lodging with a consequent reduction in pay is not within the scope of the National Insurance Contributions (NICs) definition of earnings with consequent savings for employer and employee. However, if the employee is paid a gross wage out of which a rental or deduction is made, then the employee is liable to be taxed on the whole salary.

Q3.6 **How do I handle holiday pay and entitlement in a business which closes down in the winter months?**

A. Within any statement of terms and conditions, information on holidays should be stated precisely, so that the employee is fully aware of his or her entitlement to holidays, holiday pay and accrued holiday pay on termination of employment. If there are conflicting interests or special business needs regarding when employees may take their holiday entitlement, this needs to be included in the written terms. For example, a seasonal hotel may include in its terms that all paid holiday must be taken at the end of the season, when the business closes. It is common for such businesses to put limits on the amount of holiday that can be taken at any particular time, or to employ staff only on fixed-term contracts for the season, with the understanding of minimal holiday entitlement, and the payment of accrued holiday pay on completion of the contract.

Q3.7 **How do I recover overpayments of wages?**

A. Strictly, under English law, recovery of overpayment of wages owing to a mistake is not possible. However, the **Wages Act 1986** does not actually prohibit any attempt to take such action. If the problem is not the employee's fault, and he or she has spent the money, or taken on new financial commitments, the money may not be recovered. The employee's defence is that the employer has led the employee to believe that he or she is entitled to the payment (*Avon County Council v Howlett* (1983) IRLR 171). A more recent case indicates that the appropriate defence is that the employee has in good faith changed his or her financial position as a result of the overpayment, so that it would be unfair to order recovery of the overpayment, although any amount not yet spent may be recovered (*Lipkin Gorman v Karpnale Ltd* (1992) 4 All ER 512). If it could be proved that the employee had realised the mistake before spending the money, failure to return the overpayment could lead to a prosecution under the **Theft Act 1968**. It is advisable to provide in the contract that any overpayment, whether from mistake of fact or law, can be recovered from an employee by deduction from wages due. This cannot lead to a breach of the **Wages Act 1986**.

Q3.8 **What deductions are authorised by the Wages Act 1986?**

A. The normal authorised deductions are those required by law, namely PAYE tax and National Insurance Contributions (NICs). Any other deduction must be agreed beforehand by the employee, either as part of an agreed and signed contract of employment or in some other written form. The worker's agreement to the deduction must pre-date the actual deduction (*Discount Tobacco & Confectionery Ltd v Williamson* (1993) ICR 371). Other exceptions can be the recovery of an overpayment of wages or expenses (where this is provided for in the contract of employment — see Q3.7), the result of statutory disciplinary proceedings, where the employee has taken part in a strike or other industrial action and has therefore refused to work, or to satisfy a court order or industrial tribunal decision (though even here the employee's consent should be obtained in writing). Other authorised deductions include attachment of earnings orders and Child Support Agency orders.

Q3.9 **How can I get all my employees to be paid through a bank account?**

A. The **Wages Act 1986** repealed the **Truck Act 1831** and **1860**, which imposed restrictions on the method of payment of wages, in particular that manual workers were to be paid in "coin of the realm". Therefore, the statutory right to insist on payment in cash no longer exists. However, the method of paying wages now rests as a matter for agreement between the employer and the employee. Those employees who were paid in cash before the Truck Acts were repealed (with effect from 1 January 1987) cannot be compelled to change to cheque or credit transfer. If you are determined to impose such a new payment system, then ultimately you would have to terminate the old contract of employment and offer a new one. More appropriately, it is best to consult with staff and try to persuade them that the new method is better for all concerned and obtain their written consent to such a change. If you also intend to change the frequency of payment from weekly to monthly, then you will need not only the employees' agreement but also to provide contingency plans for your employees in order to help them change their budgeting cycle. This is normally done through a system of decreasing advances on wages over a fixed period.

If difficulty is experienced in getting agreement to change of payment method or period of payment, it is normal practice to offer an incentive in terms of a one-off money payment.

Q3.10 **How can I recover cash shortages after my employees have been incompetent in handling cash?**

A.   Apart from the deductions discussed in Q3.8, there are some special rules under the **Wages Act 1986** for those employees within retail employment, including hotel and catering workers who are cash handlers or are responsible for controlling stock.

1. The employer must notify the employee of the total amount of the deduction to be made in respect of deficiencies of cash or shortages of stock and then issue a demand in writing and on pay-day.

2. Where losses are attributable, then deductions are limited to one tenth of gross wages on any particular pay-day.

3. If this deduction does not cover the entire deficiency, further deductions may be made as long as no more than one tenth of gross wages is deducted at any one time.

4. Deductions must be made within 12 months of the discovery of the shortage, and if the employee leaves there is no limit

as to the amount that can be deducted from the final pay packet, as long as it is within the 12 month period.

Q3.11 What remedies do employees have recourse to if they believe that unfair deductions have been made from their wages?

A.   All employees are entitled to a degree of protection under the **Wages Act 1986**, regardless of their length of service. In particular, industrial tribunals will hear cases where an employee believes that unlawful deductions have been made from his or her wages. Such a complaint must be made within three months of the date of the payment of the wages, unless it can be shown that to do so was practically impossible. If the complaint refers to a series of unfair deductions, then the time limit is taken from the last unlawful deduction (*Reid v Camphill Engravers* (1990) IRLR 268). If the tribunal finds that such deductions were unfair (or indeed that enforced repayments to the employer were unfair), then the employer can be forced to repay the full amount.

Q3.12 What happens regarding the payment of staff if the business fails?

A.   Employees do have certain protection under the **Insolvency Act 1986**, whereby their remuneration is given a degree of preferential debt provision, namely that up to four months' wages can be recovered. There is an upper limit on the amount which is altered from time to time. The remuneration includes all the normal elements of wages as outlined in the answer to Q3.1. However, it does not include any award for unfair dismissal, or for any notice period money that might be due after insolvency.

The employee may be able to recover further sums from the Department for Education and Employment, such as arrears of pay and accrued holiday pay, but only to a total sum of £210 per week.

Q3.13 Do I have to give equal pay to all employees when I have many different types of employees with varying lengths of service?

A. The **Equal Pay Act 1970** gives men and women the right to equal pay where they are doing like work, or work rated as equivalent or of equal value. To be successful before an industrial tribunal in a claim for equal pay, the man or woman must identify a comparator colleague: a current worker or perhaps a predecessor (eg *Hayward v Cammell Laird Shipbuilders Ltd* (1988) House of Lords IRLR 257). To avoid a claim, the most systematic and expensive approach would be to undertake a full job evaluation exercise but this may be impractical. You must be sure of your job categories within the organisation chart and of the specific responsibilities and accountabilities of the various positions. You should also look across departments for comparators, for example the responsibilities of a particular grade of chef might be deemed as being of equal value to a particular grade of receptionist. There are of course good reasons why some people in jobs of equal value might be paid at different levels, namely experience, qualifications, individual merit and length of service. However, you must be sure that these legitimate differences do exist between jobholders of different gender.

It is not, for example, sufficient to give people different job titles which really mean very little in terms of responsibility, as in a case where a waitress was paid less than a male comparator who was given the title of "banqueting supervisor" despite there being little difference between his job and that of the waitress (*Sorbie v Trust House Forte Hotels Ltd* (1977) ITR 85 EAT). However, in another case where equal value was claimed, it was clearly shown that a male canteen worker was not comparable to a female colleague because he was required to work shifts and be responsible for stock control and handling money, none of which the female employee undertook (*Capper Pass Ltd v Allan* (1980) ICR 434 HL). In a recent test case in the House of Lords, yet to be fully recorded,

North Yorkshire County Council was found to have breached the equal pay legislation when it cut the pay of "dinner ladies" following privatisation of the school meals service. The women concerned were able to show that they were then paid less than the male workers who had previously been the comparators for assessing work of equal value.

Q3.14   What elements of remuneration are counted when carrying out an analysis for equal pay purposes?

A.   For the purposes of wage calculation and comparability, the **Equal Pay Act 1970** defines pay as "basic wage plus any other consideration, either in cash or kind, which the worker receives directly or indirectly in respect of his employment from his employer". Pay therefore includes elements other than the basic wage, such as bonuses, performance-related pay, individual merit payments, and to the specific benefits of a particular job, such as company car, health insurance, travel concessions and in-company discounts. This also includes occupational pension schemes into which the employer may make contributions for the employee.

Q3.15   What arrangements must I make regarding the provision of pensions for my employees?

A.   Whilst there is universal right to the state pension in the UK based upon the individual's contribution record, the right to an additional occupational pension is determined by the employer and the written terms and conditions of the employee's contract. The particulars of any pension or pension scheme must be contained within the written statement of terms of employment, though the full details may be published elsewhere. However, if there are no pension rights, then the contract must clearly state that fact, for failure to do so can lead to problems of implied terms at any future tribunal hearing (*Eagland v British Telecommunications plc* (1992) IRLR 323 CA). Many companies now actively promote an occupational pension scheme, having "contracted out" of the second level of state pensions, the State Earnings Related Pension Scheme (SERPS). Some employers also make contributions on behalf of their employees, whilst others provide purely for contributions from the employee who may also make additional voluntary contributions (AVCs) to top up the available fund. Where an occupational pension scheme does exist, regulations under the **Social Security Act 1985** insist that full details are available to members, spouses, beneficiaries and any recognised trade unions. It is also now unlawful to exclude part-time employees from an occupational scheme on the basis that to do so would result in sex discrimination, as most part-timers are women.

Advice on setting up an occupational pension scheme may be sought from the Department for Education and Employment or from professional pension advisors.

Q3.16 **What regulations apply to personal gifts given by the employer to employees?**

A.   This question concerns personal gifts given by the employer to employees. Tips and gratuities clearly fall within the scope of the Inland Revenue, and are normally the personal responsibility of the employee, unless a "tronc" is in operation, when the supervisor of the tronc is held responsible for declaration of income.

In the case of gifts made by the employer the original approach was the so-called convertibility test whereby the gift or fringe benefit would only be considered as remuneration and liable to tax if it could be converted into cash. Gifts of £10 and under will not be subject to taxation.

Since 1988, there has been a distinction between the gifts received by directors and those earning £8500 per annum or more and those earning less than £8500. For directors and those earning £8500 per annum or more, the tax is calculated on the cost of the benefit to the employer and not, as was effectively the case, at the second-hand value. There is a rider that depreciation may be taken into account, thus estimating the gift at current market value. For those earning less than £8500 the convertibility test still applies and is therefore more favourable. Note that anything similar to a voucher which can be converted into gifts is to be avoided as the full cost will be taxable. Also if an employer reimburses the employee for prior purchase of a gift, then the full cost of the gift will be taxable.

Q3.17 **Are there any tax implications in respect of benefits and perks received by staff as part of their terms and conditions?**

A. Yes. Again, the regulations set out in the previous answer apply, and it is the duty of the employer to deduct tax from the employee's earnings for all benefits, including car and fuel allowances for travel to work, meal vouchers, private telephone bills where use is not exclusively for work, and accommodation except where it is part of the terms and conditions of the job, or is a customary provision, or for security purposes. The employer may choose not to treat all of these types of benefits as PAYE tax deductions, but must in that case annually complete form P11D for those earning £8500 or more and form P9D for those earning under £8500. Beneficial loans at attractive interest rates also come under the P11D umbrella, taxable on a cash equivalence basis amounting to an interest rate of 7.75% (from 6 March 1993). Any interest paid by the employee is deducted from the taxable amount. There are two exemptions, namely small loans where the cash equivalent does not exceed £300 in any tax year, and loans for qualifying purposes of up to £30,000 for the purchase of property which is the employee's only or main residence.

Q3.18 **What is the current situation on National Insurance Contributions (NICs)?**

A. Employers have a duty to pay NICs in respect of their employees but not in respect of self-employed persons working for them as contractors, such as window cleaners and musicians, etc (see

Q2.3). The current system was established under the **Social Security Act 1975** (as amended) to provide for sick pay, unemployment benefit, pensions, maternity pay, widowhood and industrial injuries. The level of NICs depends on the wage or salary earned and has lower and upper limits. For the tax year 1995/96 the lower limit for employees is £58 per week. For earnings less than that sum no NICs are payable. The employer's rate of contribution depends on whether the business has contracted out of the State Earnings Related Pension Scheme (SERPS). At the time of writing the maximum for an employer who has contracted out of SERPS is 10.2% on all earnings of £210 per week or more. There is an excellent freephone advisory service on current rates and practice provided by the Contributions Agency and the number can be found in your local phone book.

Q3.19 **How should I handle the payment of casual workers?**

A.   The issue of the definition of a casual worker is dealt with in Q2.6, with reference to the defining case for the hospitality industry (*O'Kelly and others v Trusthouse Forte plc* (1983) IRLR 369). On engagement of a casual worker, the employer must request the worker to complete form P46A or B before starting work so that his or her tax liabilities are met. If this is not done, it is possible that the Inland Revenue, which is well-practised in investigating hotel casual worker issues, may reclaim from the employer the tax at the standard rate on all wages paid. The employer must also endeavour to obtain from the casual worker a National Insurance number and ensure that this is noted on all pay sheets and tax forms relating to the individual.

Q3.20 **Should part-timers be paid on a pro-rata basis with full-time staff?**

A.   Recent legislation in the UK and rulings from the European Court of Justice have greatly enhanced the standing and employment rights of the ever-increasing number of part-time workers in the labour force (**Employment Protection (Part-time Employees) Regulations 1995**). In particular, there is the precedent that to treat part-timers differently from full-timers could be construed as sex discrimination against women as the majority of part-timers are female. This has been strengthened by the **Occupational Pension Schemes (Equal Access to Membership) Amendment Regulations 1995**, which make it unlawful to exclude part-timers from an occupational scheme. As a result part-time employees should enjoy, pro-rata, the same terms and conditions as full-timers. There is no justification for paying part-timers less than the basic rate for the job, other than through the normal reasons for differences in pay, such as length of service and individual merit. However, a recent European Court of Justice ruling on a German case (*Stadt Lengerich v Angelika Helmig* (1995)) confirms that overtime payments need only be at the enhanced rate (eg time and a half) once the hours worked go beyond the normal hours worked by full-time colleagues.

Q3.21 **Do any regulations pertaining to Sunday trading affect the hospitality industry?**

A. The **Sunday Trading Act 1994** enabled shops to open legally for various hours on Sundays. Employees were given the right to refuse to work on that day except where they are contracted to work on Sundays only. As the hospitality industry has always tended to be a seven day working week, the implications are limited. However, many larger hotels do have retail outlets within their business and therefore may be affected. In such cases, employees must not be dismissed for refusing to work on a Sunday, must not be selected for redundancy on that basis, and must not suffer in any other way, such as loss of benefits or chances of promotion and development. With the more recent relaxation of the Sunday licensing laws (6 August 1995), many more bar staff in pubs, restaurants and hotels may be required to work through Sunday afternoon. When employing staff, employers should make it clear in written statements of terms and conditions when employees may be required to work and how rotas are formulated, and should generally consult existing staff on attitudes to working on Sundays. Your statement of main terms and conditions of work should also set out in detail any payments for Sunday working.

Q3.22 **How should I deal with the administration of service charges and tipping?**

A.   With regard to service charges, this additional charge on a customer's bill is tending to disappear, as hospitality managers increasingly include all extra charges, VAT as well, in the full price of the item. This was encouraged by the **Consumer Protection Act 1987**, which advised incorporation of all elements in the one price, stating that exactly what is included in the price advertised must be clearly displayed on menus inside and outside the establishment. If a service charge is still in operation and if all or part of the service charge raised is distributed to the staff, the management/employer is responsible for making the deduction of income tax, and reporting and paying all sums to the Inland Revenue.

Tipping is left very much to the discretion of the customer. If staff keep their own tips, then it is the individuals' responsibility to declare the amount for taxation purposes. If a tronc exists, that is where all monies received as tips are pooled and divided on some pre-agreed system, then the person in charge of the tronc (eg a restaurant manager) must make the declarations to the Inland Revenue. If a tronc system exists, you should ensure that the points system on which it is distributed is fair and understood by all workers affected, and is not changed without consultation.

Q3.23 **What PAYE records must I maintain?**

A.   Table 2 itemises the forms or items concerning PAYE, their purpose and the date they should be returned to the Inland Revenue following the end of the tax year on 5 April. (These are in addition to the regular monthly or quarterly returns and payments to be made to the Inland Revenue.)

Table 2: PAYE Records

Form/Item	Purpose	Date Due
PAYE	Payment of outstanding income tax and NICs relating to the immediately preceding tax year	19 April
P14/60	Year end summary of tax and NIC deductions for each employee	19 May
P35	Employer's reconciliation of PAYE deductions for all employees	19 May
P9D	Benefits in kind return for employees earning less than £8500 per annum	6 June
P11D	Benefits in kind return for all directors and employees earning £8500 or more per annum	6 June
CLASS 1A NIC	Additional employer's NICs relating to company cars	19 June

There are stiff penalties, up to £3000 or more in some circumstances, for late returns, and employers must keep in touch with their tax office to ensure they know the forthcoming deadlines for each tax year.

Q3.24　**What is the present situation regarding minimum wages in the hospitality industry now that the Wages Councils have been abolished?**

A.　Although the Wages Councils were phased out for the hotel and catering industry following the **Wages Act 1986**, their influence may still be felt. Whilst all those under 21 are in no way affected, if an employee was employed before 30 August 1993 at the then minimum, £2.92 per hour, that minimum would be an implied minimum wage under the individual's contract of employment, and to reduce it would be a breach of contract unless mutually agreed. However, in most cases now, and for all employees taken on since 30 August 1993, the employer is free to set whatever wage rates he or she desires. Clearly, good employers will be aware of the competitor rates in other parts of the hospitality industry and also in other industries competing for the labour force. The aspect of equal pay may also have a bearing, as in the case of a new female worker comparing her wage with that of a male comparator who was employed before 1993.

Q3.25 **What legal obligations does an employer in the hospitality industry have to provide transport for female employees or to accompany them home when they finish work after 11.00pm?**

A. There is no such statutory obligation. Under s.6 of the **Sex Discrimination Act 1975** a condition or benefit applied to one sex should be applied to both. To offer any benefit including transport would be discriminatory unless this facility were offered to both sexes. Subjectively, an employer may argue that a female employee is more vulnerable, but all the statistics of physical assaults show that the most likely victims are males in their early twenties.

Q3.26 **Am I permitted to collect union dues from my employees' pay?**

A. Many workers who are union members pay their subscriptions by "check off" arrangements, ie the employer deducts the amount due and then pays it to the union. This can only be done where the employee/union member has given his or her written consent within the last three years and has not withdrawn it. The authorisation must be dated and signed by the employee. Authorisation lapses after three years if it is not renewed.

4. SICKNESS

Q4.1   Am I obliged to provide sick pay?

A.   Employees are not automatically entitled to sick pay unless the contract of employment specifically states that this benefit is applicable. Employers are, however, obliged to pay Statutory Sick Pay (SSP) (see Q4.2). In the absence of clear agreement as to how long the sick pay benefit will last, this will be for a reasonable period only (*Howman & Son v Blyth* (1983) IRLR 139).

Q4.2   How do I handle Statutory Sick Pay (SSP) arrangements for new and existing employees?

A.   Most employees, including part-timers, are entitled to SSP and there is no minimum service qualification. Non-qualifying employees include those over 65 years, those with a contract of employment of less than 12 weeks and pregnant employees from the 11th week before expected confinement, for the following 18 weeks after the birth. To qualify for SSP, the employee must be incapable of carrying out normal duties and be incapacitated for four or more consecutive working days.

All employees must be given details of SSP, preferably within the written statement of terms and conditions. The following points should be included.

- If an employee was given a form SSP1(L) by his or her previous employer, this must be given to the new supervisor or personnel department.
- In the case of absence caused by sickness, the employee will be entitled to SSP. The rate will be in accordance with the current scales and regulations.
- For the purposes of calculating SSP, the working week is as stated in the terms and conditions.

- Where an employee receives both SSP and company sick pay benefit, the total will not exceed the normal basic wage.

- If the SSP entitlement is exceeded (beyond 28 weeks), but the employee still qualifies for company benefit, he or she will be asked to declare the amount received from the DSS and this will be deducted from his or her wage. The employer must complete form SSP1 for the employee.

- The rules relating to SSP are available from the DSS.

- A period of incapacity for work (PIW) is defined as any period of four or more consecutive days, including rest days. Where PIWs are separated by not more than two weeks, they are considered as one period, known as "linking". In such cases the employee does not need to requalify by being absent for another three waiting days (the first three days of sickness when no SSP is paid).

- On termination of employment, the employer completes form SSP1(L) for each employee.

Q4.3 **What details should I give my staff about sickness schemes?**

A. The right of an employee to receive payment when sick depends very much on the terms and conditions of employment. If a company sickness scheme exists, then full details must be itemised in the written statement of main terms and conditions (**Employment Protection (Consolidation) Act 1978**, s.1). If no express term within the contract exists, there is no presumption in favour of payment, and previous custom and practice will be taken into consideration by a court, unless a specific agreement has been entered into (*Mears v Safecar Security Ltd* (1982) IRLR 183). However, under the Statutory Sick Pay (SSP) scheme, the **Social Security Contributions and Benefits Act 1992** amended 1982 legislation which introduced SSP and placed an obligation on all employers to provide SSP to all qualifying employees. The employer may be responsible for up to 28 weeks' SSP in any one year, at the prevailing rates, though smaller employers (those with National Insurance Contributions (NICs) of less than £20,000 in the last tax year) may be able to off-set SSP payments against their NICs.

The best practice is for an employer to give full details of any company schemes in the contract of employment, leaving the employee in no doubt as to his or her rights. Entitlement should be spelt out by confirming the company scheme procedures and the qualifying rules, and also the procedures for SSP. Regarding company schemes, it is important to inform the employee of the benefit in number of weeks' pay dependent on length of service, the reporting procedure for the employee to follow if sick, and details of the self-certification scheme (see Q4.5).

Q4.4 **What action should I take in the case of an employee who has been absent through sickness on a long-term basis?**

A. If the sickness or injury is so serious that performing normal duties is impossible, then frustration of contract may apply. An example of frustration of contract is the case of the employee who was disqualified from driving when that very task was the purpose of the job (*Williams v Watsons Luxury Coaches Ltd* (1990) IRLR 164 EAT). However, for most cases it is a more delicate matter of whether the job can be kept open for an employee with a long-term illness. For many small businesses this could be a crucial issue. The employer must take into consideration the status, capability and length of service of the employee and the possibility of alternative employment. However, remember that an employer may contact an employee's doctor only if the employee gives written consent (**Access to Medical Reports Act 1988**). Close contact must be maintained with the employee and if dismissal is likely, then a period of consultation and warning of the outcome must take place. Whether company scheme or SSP (for which the limit is 28 weeks), sickness benefit schemes must be followed. Proper notice of termination, within the terms of the contract, must be given.

Q4.5   What are the guidelines for a self-certification procedure on sickness?

A.   Since June 1982, a self-certification scheme has been in operation whereby doctors do not issue medical certificates for up to and including the first seven days' absence from work. Most companies have therefore introduced a self-certification procedure which takes the form of a company benefits claim. Following a period of sickness absence, the employee must complete a self-certification form on his or her return to work. The form should include full details of the absence as confirmed by the supervisor, and the employee must give details of the illness. Longer periods of sickness must be supported by a medical certificate and the employee must return to work only when he or she has been signed off by the doctor, as being fit to return. Employers can insist on a doctor's medical certificate from the first day of absence through sickness if it is felt that an employee is abusing the system.

Q4.6   What measures can I take against an employee who regularly has a single day's absence from duty?

A.   The hospitality industry has traditionally suffered from a high level of absenteeism, very often of short duration, which is perhaps caused by the pressures and lifestyle of many catering workers. Such absences, even a day, must be formally recorded, and any regularity or pattern identified. The self-certification process must be enforced, and if problems do arise, the individual and, where appropriate, the supervisor should be spoken to, and the health and absence record of the individual discussed. The spirit of any counselling discussions must be positive and constructive. Some form of joint action should be agreed with the employee, such as a commitment to a proper medical check-up or a review of his or her satisfaction with the job and its environment. It may be necessary to commence disciplinary action, such as giving a warning about the amount of sick leave and stating what future behaviour is acceptable and expected.

5. MATERNITY ISSUES

Q5.1   **What time off for antenatal care must I give a pregnant employee?**

A.   All pregnant employees, regardless of length of service or hours of work, are entitled to a reasonable amount of time off work for antenatal care, as set out in the **Employment Act 1980**. It is important to note that antenatal care should be distinguished from sickness during pregnancy, and is normally concerned with the woman's appointments at a hospital or clinic prior to the birth. These usually begin between the 8th and 12th week of pregnancy and thereafter at monthly intervals, although this does depend on the particular health and circumstances of each woman. Towards the last two months of pregnancy, the frequency of visits to a clinic may well increase to one every two weeks. The employee should request the time off, and should not be refused unreasonably. There is also a precedent to include relaxation classes under the banner of antenatal care, if this is recommended by a medical advisor (*Gregory v Tudsbury* (1982) IRLR 267).

Industrial tribunals invariably find in favour of the employee if the employer feels the incidence and timing of appointments is unreasonable, especially if medical advisors have recommended such visits. The employer has the duty to ask to see, and the employee the duty to produce, both a certificate of pregnancy (Mat B1) at the start, and all subsequent appointment cards, with the onus being on the employer to request the production of such evidence.

Q5.2   **What is the situation if an employee who works only two or three days a week asks for one or more of these days off for antenatal care?**

A.   There is nothing specific in the law covering such a situation, nor are there any precedents. The employer would have to be extremely careful in refusing such a request and would have to consider the reasons why the employee concerned cannot attend antenatal care on the days she does not work.

Q5.3 **What is the current situation regarding maternity leave?**

A.   Since the EC Pregnant Workers Directive came into effect in October 1994, all pregnant workers, regardless of length of service or hours of service per week, are entitled to 14 weeks' maternity leave, commencing at any point during the 11 weeks prior to the expected date of childbirth.

During this short-term period of maternity leave, all contractual rights must be maintained, for example holiday entitlement, company benefits and pension scheme contributions by the employer. The employer must pay Statutory Maternity Pay (SMP). The 14 weeks' leave may be extended due to certified medical reasons, or if the baby is born late.

The employee must give at least 21 days' notice of her intention to commence maternity leave, except where premature birth renders this impossible, and she must produce a certificate of pregnancy from a doctor or midwife.

If the employee becomes absent from work on pregnancy-related grounds after the sixth week before the expected date of childbirth, the employer can insist that the period of maternity leave commences from the date of absence.

The woman does not need to give the employer notification of her return to work unless she wishes to return earlier than the 14 weeks, in which case she must give seven days' notice. The employer may postpone the return by seven days.

Women with two or more years' service still qualify for the full period of long-term maternity leave, 40 weeks in all, made up of up to 11 weeks before the due date and up to 29 weeks after the birth, commencing with the week in which the baby is born.

It is very important that employers follow the procedures carefully and with due care and consideration. Industrial tribunals consider the onus of proper conduct, for example with the notification clauses, as lying with the employer.

The new legislation gives all women, regardless of length of service, the right not to be dismissed on purely maternity-related grounds, with the exception of a case of legitimate redundancy.

Q5.4   Is an employee entitled to return to work after maternity leave?

A.   An employee entitled to short-term maternity leave of 14 weeks, or an employee with two years' service entitled to 40 weeks' maternity leave has a right to return to work after that period to the same job, provided that when giving 21 days' notice of her intention to start maternity leave, she states her intention to return. If, on account of redundancy, she cannot return to her old job, she must be offered a suitable alternative position on terms and conditions not substantially less favourable. She must still give the employer notification that she intends to return to work, and, at least 21 days beforehand, notice of her proposed date of return.

The return to work may be postponed by the employee by up to four weeks on a medical certificate, and the employer may postpone her return by up to four weeks also, owing to specified reasons. The reasons must be notified to the employee, and may be owing to the general business requirements of the employer and not necessarily limited to the circumstances connected with the maternity leave. Any extension of the four week period must be by agreement between employer and employee, otherwise a dismissal may be deemed to have taken place. Employers can no longer seek confirmation of the intention to return until after the 11th week after the birth of the baby.

Q5.5 **Does an employee on maternity leave continue to have full use of all benefits, including a company car?**

A.   Where a woman is on the short-term maternity leave period of 14 weeks, she is entitled to all contractual rights during the maternity leave period, as if she were not absent. Short-term maternity leave is viewed in the same way as paid annual leave. Thus a company car, if part of the non-remuneration package, should continue to be supplied, as should the continuation of employers' pension contributions and the accrual of holiday pay and any other contractual benefits.

For women on long-term maternity leave (ie of up to 40 weeks), the situation is less clear cut, and very much depends on the joint actions of the employer and employee, and what has been agreed, whether expressly or implied. The retention of the P45 or the employee being kept on the payroll would clearly indicate that the contract of employment is continuing. The advice is for the parties to be quite clear, and have written agreement, about such significant matters as a company car, otherwise it may be that in law the contract is suspended during the time of the maternity leave (*Institute of the Motor Industry v Harvey* (1992) IRLR 343). However, it could be considered to be sex discrimination if a woman on maternity leave is treated any differently from a man on sick leave. In the case of *Reay v Sunderland Health Authority* (unreported), the tribunal held that a woman on maternity leave should have received time off in lieu for bank holidays because male workers on sick leave had been entitled to time off in lieu.

Q5.6 **What is the difference between Statutory Maternity Pay (SMP) and the Maternity Allowance (MA)?**

A.   Statutory Maternity Pay (SMP) is payable to all employees who have 26 weeks of continuous service at the 15th week (the "Qualifying Week") before the expected date of childbirth, have stopped working owing to pregnancy, have average earnings above the lower limit, and have given the necessary 21 days' notice of intention to stop work owing to pregnancy, as well as providing medical evidence of the expected week of childbirth. Beginning at any time from the 11th week before the expected week of birth, the SMP lasts for 18 weeks. At the time of going to print, current rates were 90% of the average weekly earnings for the first 6 weeks, and £52.50 for up to 12 weeks thereafter.

Maternity Allowance (MA) is payable to women not eligible for SMP, such as those with less than 26 weeks of continuous service with the current employer. Payable for up to 18 weeks, the employee must have paid National Insurance Contributions (NICs) for at least 26 weeks in the 66 weeks immediately prior to the expected week of childbirth. MA is not liable to income tax and NICs, and the employer, having established that the employee is not eligible for SMP, must provide the employee with the maternity certificate and form SMP1 within seven days. Payment is via the Department of Social Security.

Q5.7 **What records must I maintain regarding maternity pay?**

A. Records must be kept for three years after the tax year to which the records refer. You should maintain records as follows:

- the weeks for which SMP was paid
- the amount of SMP paid in each week
- the dates and reasons for any non-payments
- the maternity certificates (Mat B1) submitted
- copies of any Mat B1 forms where the originals have been returned once SMP liability has finished.

As SMP is to be regarded as earnings for social security purposes, the employer must also deduct PAYE and National Insurance Contributions (NICs), so records must also be kept for the Inland Revenue for claims of reimbursement to be made:

- record SMP payments on the employee's Deduction Working Sheets (P11)

- record the total SMP payments on the employer's end of year returns (P14)
- record the total gross SMP payments and the total sum of NICs on the Annual Statement (P35).

Q5.8 Who pays Statutory Maternity Pay (SMP)?

A.   Payments are made by the employer in the same way as any earnings, but 92% is recoverable. Small employers who pay £20,000 or less annually in gross National Insurance Contributions (NICs) qualify for Small Employers' Relief and may recover 100% of SMP. The 92% sum is arrived at by deducting the amount paid from the total amount of NICs and tax paid to the Inland Revenue every month.

6. HEALTH AND SAFETY AT WORK

Q6.1 **As an employer, what are my responsibilities under common law for health and safety matters?**

A.   Though much health and safety legislation is now under statute, some key common law and civil liability issues remain, of which employers should be aware. The common law duty requires employers to ensure a safe and healthy place of work, safe plant, appliances and equipment within the workplace, the employment of trained and competent persons, and a safe system of work. All the employer's activities should also be carried out within a duty of care, or civil liability, which ensures that employees are kept safe and healthy in the place of work. If the employer is found to be negligent, then damages may be sought in a civil court, where the employee must prove a causal connection between the breach of duty of care and the injuries sustained.

Q6.2 **Who is affected by the Health and Safety at Work Act 1974, particularly regarding the issue of personal responsibility?**

A.   All people at work are covered by the Act, including employers, employees and the self-employed. The only exception is domestic servants in a private house. It is also important to note that the legislation is designed to ensure the safety and health of the general public, notably customers in the hospitality industry. Employers have a responsibility towards every individual (whether employee or customer), and must have knowledge of the particular employee, his or her abilities, frailties and characteristics (*Paris v Stepney Borough Council* (1951) 1 AER 42). Employers also have a duty towards the employees of independent contractors whilst they are on the premises. Furthermore, employees have a duty to take reasonable care to avoid injury to themselves and others by their work and actions, and must co-operate with the employer over these matters. The general point is that everyone can be held personally responsible for the work they do and, if found negligent, can be prosecuted. Serious offences can lead to fines of up to £20,000 and up to two years' imprisonment.

Q6.3 **What key points should I communicate to employees about the Health and Safety at Work Act 1974?**

A. Staff should be aware that the business has a health and safety policy (a requirement for those firms with five or more employees) and be given notice of any changes and additions. In particular, the employer should highlight certain aspects that affect the employee. The element of personal responsibility, outlined in Q6.2, is clearly one area to be stressed. Employers must ensure that all employees, whether temporary or permanent (note this also applies to part-time and casual workers) must receive adequate training, instruction and supervision in their work, and be kept fully informed of risks that might affect them and of what to do to reduce those risks. Training in health and safety is recommended by code of practice and required by law under the **Fire Precautions Act 1971**. Where appropriate it is also important for employers to warn staff that the use of protective clothing and equipment is essential, by pointing out the possible consequences of not doing so (*Pape v Cumbria County Council* (1992) 3 All ER 211). Employers should ensure that there is an effective flow of information to all staff, that communication on health and safety matters is efficient, and that safety representatives, where they exist, are properly trained and committed to their pivotal role of communicating all relevant matters. It may also be prudent to inform staff that they must not be afraid to use their initiative in potentially dangerous situations.

Dismissal is automatically unfair if the actions for which an employee was dismissed were a result of avoiding imminent danger at work, or he or she was carrying out recognised duties in connection with health and safety.

Q6.4   How is the Health and Safety at Work Act 1974 enforced?

A.   Inspectors may be appointed by the Health and Safety Executive (HSE) or by local authorities; the prime responsibility of these inspectors is to ensure that places of work are complying with all relevant health and safety legislation. Inspectors have right of entry, and the power to remove documents, materials and equipment and to take samples and photographs. They can take immediate action to make safe a dangerous situation, and can carry out full investigations. The inspectors can also issue improvement notices requiring certain corrective action to be carried out by particular dates, or prohibition notices banning certain activities and the use of certain equipment, etc.

Many hotel and catering businesses have developed very good working relationships with local inspectors and environmental health officers (EHOs) by adopting a mature and constructive approach to making improvements. In serious cases of breaches of the legislation or failure to carry out improvement notices, the inspectors do have the power to stop the business trading until the changes have been completed. Appeals against notices can be lodged but the tribunal is likely to be impressed by the expertise of the inspector (*Bellhaven Brewery Co. Ltd v McClean* (1975) IRLR 370). If all notices have failed then prosecution may result, with fines on conviction of up to £20,000 and imprisonment of up to two years for certain serious offences.

It is also important to note that the concept of corporate offences is now regularly considered by the courts, whereby the negligent actions of one individual, perhaps a supervisor or junior manager, would be considered to have emanated from the direction of more senior management, as embodied by the company (*Tesco Stores Ltd v Nattrass* (1971) 2 All ER 127). In extreme cases resulting in death, this has been considered as "corporate manslaughter" with directors held personally responsible. One such case is a canoeing trip that was so poorly organised that four young people died. The managing director of the company responsible was found guilty of manslaughter and jailed for three years.

Q6.5 **What are the implications for my business of the recent Management of Health and Safety Regulations 1992?**

A.   These regulations came into effect in January 1993 and were aimed at a general improvement in the management of health and safety issues. Principally, they require employers to adopt a systematic approach to identifying the risks within their workplace and then take whatever action is appropriate to prevent accidents that could result. A summary of the key requirements follows.

1.   Carry out a "risk assessment" to assess all health and safety risks in the workplace, record findings and take preventative action. The types of risks most likely to be found in the hospitality industry include lifting, slipping, cutting, burns and the use of dangerous equipment.

2.   Appoint sufficient and competent personnel from the workforce to assist, and ensure that they are trained to assess risks and take action. Include the surveillance of health-endangering activities that generate noise, fumes and harmful substances.

3.   Plan emergency procedures and carry out practice drills, eg fire and bomb threat evacuation procedures.

4.   Ensure that all staff, including temporary workers such as casuals and contract catering staff (see Q6.7) are given full information, training and supervision regarding the specific risks associated with their area of work. Ensure that information is available to all parties concerned, and ensure co-operation and co-ordination with others such as the contract catering staff employer, who may be on the premises.

Q6.6   **What health and safety regulations affect me as an employer with regard to the working environment?**

A.   The 1992 health and safety regulations, often referred to as the "six pack", are the main regulations concerned with health and safety at work. There is not the space here to deal with all the details (instead see section 3 of *Croner's Catering*), but employers should ensure they understand the following points.

1.   The **Provision and Use of Work Equipment Regulations 1992** make the employer responsible for the suitability of the equipment in use, its maintenance in good safe working order, the identification of special risks attached to any equipment, and the training and instruction of all employees involved in the use, supervision and management of the work processes. Catering enterprises have a great deal of equipment, much of it electrical and potentially dangerous, so check everything is in accordance with these regulations, and obtain more information from the Health and Safety Executive (HSE).

2.   The **Manual Handling Operations Regulations 1992** require that proper risk assessment is carried out with regard to hazardous manual handling, for example the carrying of heavy items over wet or slippery floors. Alternative methods of transporting such goods should be reviewed, such as the use of trolleys, and staff should be trained in how to lift properly with less risk of serious back injury, which is a major cause of long-term sickness absence in all industries.

3.   The **Workplace (Health, Safety and Welfare) Regulations 1992** cover workplace conditions such as lighting, ventilation and suitability of seating and work areas. There are considerations concerning temperatures in indoor work areas, cleanliness and the disposal of waste, the dimensions of work areas and floors, windows and pathways around the work areas as well as basic sanitary and washing facilities. There

are also provisions regarding drinking water, lockers, changing rooms and facilities for rest and eating.

4. The **Personal Protective Equipment at Work Regulations 1992** require employers to review the suitability and provision of protective clothing and apparatus and staff should be given appropriate training concerning their use. Footwear is of particular significance for catering operations.

5. The **Health and Safety (Display Screen Equipment) Regulations 1992** require employers to review the suitability of VDU workers' areas, from safety of the equipment to seating and ventilation. As more and more hospitality work is computerised, for example reservations systems, so these regulations will increase in significance. There is particular reference to planned breaks for staff who may otherwise spend too many hours looking intently at a VDU screen. Eye tests may need to be provided. As with many of these measures, care and action can lead to less sickness absence owing to migraines, eye strain and other related ailments.

Q6.7   **As a contract caterer, how am I affected by the 1992 Regulations on health and safety?**

A.   Under the **Management of Health and Safety Regulations 1992** a contractor becomes responsible for the safety of his or her staff on another's premises. As a contractor you should be certain that the equipment your staff works with is in safe working order. You must ensure that all staff, including casual event staff for example, are fully trained and instructed in the operation of equipment and other systems in the workplace. This clearly requires a lot of co-operation between the event organiser or contractor and the owner of the premises, so that staff are informed as to the risks prevalent in a particular workplace. Your responsibility also extends to any transport you provide to take contract staff to events and other locations. If you provide the transport, such as a coach, check the safety and maintenance of the vehicle and be sure that the driver is qualified and holds the appropriate licences.

Q6.8   What exactly is repetitive strain injury (RSI)?

A.   This is the term given to the accepted medical condition whereby the continuous repetition of certain physical tasks can lead to permanent injury and possible disability. It is also known as upper limb disorder (ULD). Most problems occur where insufficient and infrequent breaks are available, or where seating and height of workstations are inappropriate to the individual. Employers who ignore the complaints from staff, who do not warn staff of the risks and who do not provide proper breaks and appropriate work areas may find themselves paying out large sums in compensation (*McSherry and Lodge v British Telecommunications plc* (1992) 13 Med LR 129). One example in the hospitality industry might be the assembly line style of catering operation for airline meals.

Q6.9   Should I be concerned about recent legislation on the reporting of dangerous occurrences and the control of dangerous substances?

A.   Yes. It is a legal requirement under the **Reporting of Injuries, Diseases and Dangerous Occurrences Regulations 1985** (RIDDOR) that written records of reportable accidents and dangerous occurrences (ie those which must be reported to the appropriate enforcing authority such as the environmental health officer (EHO)) must be kept for a minimum of three years. The following must be reported:

- fatal accidents
- major injury accidents, eg fractures of skull, arm, wrist
- dangerous occurrences, eg wall collapse though no one hurt
- accidents causing more than three days' incapacity for work
- certain work-related diseases, eg dysentery or salmonella poisoning in a kitchen

- incidents relating to the gas supply.

More details are available in *Croner's Catering*, section 3.

The **Control of Substances Hazardous to Health Regulations 1988** (COSHH) came into effect on 1 October 1989 and were updated in 1994. They place a duty on employers to reduce employee exposure to dangerous substances. An assessment should be carried out of the risk of skin contact and absorption, and inhalation of the many potentially dangerous cleaning materials and chemicals used in hotels and restaurants. Examples could be oven cleaner, bleach and drain-cleaning fluids. The systematic assessment procedure must be adhered to and should include a review of all dust, fumes, vapours and gases generated around the premises. Consult *Croner's Catering Records and Procedures*, page 5-8. From HMSO you can obtain a leaflet entitled "COSHH Assessments".

Q6.10 **What level of first aid cover must I provide, and does it apply to guests as well?**

A. The **Health and Safety First Aid Regulations 1981** make the employer responsible for ensuring that adequate and appropriate equipment and facilities are provided to enable first aid to be rendered to employees if they are injured or become ill at work. There is no obligation under this legislation to take account of non-employees, although this can clearly be done on a voluntary basis. As a guideline, the number of first aiders needed during normal working hours is one trained person for every 50 employees. An appointed person who will take charge of the situation in the absence of a first aider must be available at all times. It is good practice to attempt to ensure a trained person is always available, especially at night, so perhaps consider training a night porter for this purpose. The number of properly stocked first aid boxes should be sufficient to allow ready access to all employees at work, and details on contents can be obtained from *Croner's Catering*, page

3-106. There is also a code of practice, "First Aid at Work", available from HMSO. In addition, there is a legal requirement to keep a full record in an accident book of any first aid treatment administered, as well as a detailed description of any accident. Serious accidents must be reported under the **Reporting of Injuries, Diseases and Dangerous Occurrences Regulations 1985** (RIDDOR) (see also Q6.9).

Q6.11 **What are the proper procedures when dealing with infectious diseases?**

A.   Under the **Food Safety (General Food Hygiene) Regulations 1995** there is a requirement that any person engaged in the handling of food who becomes aware that he or she is suffering from or is a carrier of any of the conditions noted below, shall immediately inform the employer or representative, who must in turn notify the appropriate medical health officer for the area. The specific conditions are:

* typhoid
* paratyphoid
* salmonella infections
* amoebic dysentery
* bacillary dysentery
* any staphylococcal infection likely to cause food poisoning, eg septic cuts, boils, spots, burns or throat or nasal infections.

Q6.12 **What procedures can I introduce to insist that all employees have medical checks and are tested for HIV?**

A.   Though reasonable to ask for personal information on health in the form of a confidential, general health questionnaire, and reasonable to insist on a medical before the start of employment, there are implications to be aware of under Article 8 of the European Convention on Human Rights. This dictates that an individual has a right to respect for his or her private life, and this includes the right to secrecy over a matter of health (*X v Commission of the European Communities* (1995) IRLR 320: ECJ). In this case, a job applicant refused an HIV test as part of the compulsory medical examination, but secretly, such a test occurred. It is worth noting that the European Court of Justice did express approval of employment-conditional medical examinations, but declared that Article 8 had been breached in this case.

In the absence of an express contractual term, a person with HIV or AIDS is not under an obligation to reveal this unless not to do so would put others at risk of harm or infection, thus breaching s.7 of the **Health and Safety at Work Act 1974**. An employer could make it a condition of employment that a candidate will need to undergo a medical at the employer's expense within a certain period of taking up duties, particularly where aspects of the job make this desirable. In most cases, however, a health questionnaire is considered more than sufficient. This should occur at the recruitment/induction process, and be part of an overall occupational health policy. Some companies do include a clause on their questionnaire that as a result of the information given, the employer may refer the applicant to a company doctor for examination. Catering firms may also introduce a Food Handlers' Declaration regarding certain infectious diseases (see Q6.11) which, if contracted, must be reported before commencing any food-related work.

Q6.13   How am I affected by occupiers' liability?

A.   The increasing availability of leisure facilities in hotels brings with it a need to be aware of the concept of occupiers' liability: that the occupier of premises must take reasonable measures to ensure the safety of the premises' equipment. Examples would most commonly be sunbeds, solaria and swimming pools. If you have such facilities you should contact your local environmental health officer (EHO) as different local authorities have brought out a variety of guidance notes and even by-laws concerning these items. These deal with proper installation, the operation by trained individuals, the availability of safety equipment, proper warnings to users of the possible damaging side effects of improper use, and the correct monitoring and analysis of the equipment, including a chemical analysis of swimming pools for quality and sterilent levels. Even if you subcontract your leisure facilities to a specialist firm, you should check on the thoroughness of their procedures for the safety of your customers. Ultimately, the occupier of the premises remains liable.

Q6.14 Can an employer be liable for an employee's stress level?

A.   While stress and psychological injury have been serious issues for employers and employees for some time, a recent case has promoted stress at work to a much higher profile. *Walker v Northumberland County Council* (1995) IRLR 35 resulted in a successful claim of unfair dismissal against the employer based on the employer's duty of care.

Mr Walker suffered two nervous breakdowns within a year. After returning to work following a period of absence because of the first breakdown, additional assistance was provided but then withdrawn after one month. The High Court decided that the Council was not responsible for the first mental illness but was responsible for the second; it was reasonably foreseeable that if Mr Walker was again exposed to the same workload further problems with his health would occur. The Council was in breach of its duty of care and the Court ruled that an employer owes a duty to employees not to cause them psychiatric damage by the volume or character of the work they are required to perform. This "duty of care" will depend upon:

– the nature of the relationship

– the magnitude of the risk of injury which was reasonably fore-seeable

- the seriousness of the consequences for the person to whom the duty is owed of the risk occurring and the cost and practicability of preventing the risk

- the practicability of remedial measures which must take into account resources and facilities at the disposal of the employer.

The Health and Safety Executive (HSE) has recently issued a guide for employers which outlines the main causes of occupational stress and sets out steps that employers can take to prevent harmful levels of stress in their organisations. The guide will make it harder for employers to claim they could not have foreseen the harmful effects of stress.

Q6.15 I am considering introducing a policy regarding smoking at work. What should I be aware of?

A.   Whilst smoking by staff in hotel and catering front of house areas is clearly controlled by both legal statute and propriety considerations, the issue of smoking in areas such as offices, canteens and other communal sites is worthy of close consideration. With the concerns over passive smoking and recent large compensation payments being awarded to sufferers, it is highly relevant to consider a business-wide smoking policy. In practice, it is best to approach this issue on a consultative and constructive basis. Perhaps a working party made up of individuals from all levels within the firm, could canvass opinion and propose recommendations. The need for a designated smoking area is one common solution, but lack of ventilation and facilities can often lead to groups of employees at the back of the hotel taking their "smoke breaks".

Another approach is to encourage each work area to determine its own guidelines whilst making all communal and eating areas strictly non-smoking. Case law has so far supported employers who, after consultation with employees, have introduced reasonable no smoking rules (*Dryden v Greater Glasgow Health Board*

(1992) IRLR 469) and found against employers who do not respond to the dangers of passive smoking (*Bland v Stockport Borough Council* 1993).

7. HARASSMENT

Q7.1   **When does a remark or act by one employee to another become a case of sexual harassment?**

A.   Section 4A of the **Public Order Act 1986** makes all forms of harassment (race, sex or disability) criminal where it is intentional.

Whilst a dictionary definition of harassment may suggest a continuing or repeated act, a single remark or act may be of sufficient seriousness to amount to a "detriment" to one sex under s.6(2)(b) of the **Sex Discrimination Act 1975**. This point was clarified in the case of *Institu Cleaning Co Ltd v Heads* (1995) IRLR 4. When a remark was made by a manager to Mrs Heads about her breasts, she resigned and claimed unlawful sex discrimination as a result of this incident. The employer argued that the remark was not sex-related, as a similar remark could have been made to a man, for example about a balding head. The Employment Appeal Tribunal (EAT) rejected this, saying that one remark was sexual and the other was not. The employer also argued that conduct cannot be "unwanted" until it had occurred and been rejected. The EAT also rejected this claim because it said that this would be a licence for harassment as a man could always argue that every act of harassment was different from the last and he was testing to see if it was wanted! The EC Recommendation and Code of Practice on Sexual Harassment refer to "unwanted conduct". The code does therefore allow for the freedom of choice by the individual to decide what behaviour, and from whom, she or he finds acceptable.

Q7.2   **When does a remark or act by one employee to another become a case of sexual harassment, for example at a Christmas party off the premises?**

A.   As stated in Q7.1, certain remarks may constitute a criminal offence. Whether the employer was considered to be vicariously liable is likely to depend upon whether the event was deemed to be in the "course of employment". It may also depend upon the extent to which the employer prohibited that mode of behaviour during normal working hours. It would also depend on whether it had been an isolated incident or whether there had been other similiar incidents during work.

Q7.3 **To what extent is it the employer's responsibility to prevent or control an individual employee's behaviour if it is discriminatory?**

A.   There is no express provision in the **Public Order Act 1986** in respect of the employer. However, under s.41 of the **Sex Discrimination Act 1975** and s.32 of the **Race Relations Act 1976** employers are vicariously liable for the discriminatory actions of their employees if those actions occur in the course of employment, even if the employer has no knowledge of, or has not sanctioned, those actions. Employers may be able to show that they are not liable if reasonable, practical steps have been taken to prevent discriminatory acts by employees. It is therefore in an employer's interest to take preventative measures, such as having a clear policy against harassment and making it clear to employees that it is a serious disciplinary offence.

Q7.4 **How should a complaint from an employee that a colleague is "calling them names" be dealt with?**

A.   The normal procedure for a grievance should be followed. Whether on the grounds of sex or race, the question of detriment must be borne in mind, ie neither employee must be treated less favourably than the other. A full, fair investigation must be carried out following the complaint which should result in adequate steps being taken to ensure that the two employees can continue their employment satisfactorily. This may involve the transfer of one or other employee to another department if possible (however, this could possibly involve breach of contract or constructive dismissal issues).

8. RECORDS, REFERENCES AND DATA PROTECTION

Q8.1 **Does the law specify any records that I am obliged to keep regarding my employees?**

A.   There are some records that you are obliged to keep by law. These are:

- Pay As You Earn (PAYE) and National Insurance records
- Statutory Maternity Pay (SMP) and Statutory Sick Pay (SSP) records
- Reporting of Injuries, Diseases and Dangerous Occurrences Regulations (RIDDOR) records (see Q6.9).

Other than these, in case of any unfair dismissal claims or similar actions, you are advised to keep:

- a copy of any contract of employment
- a copy of any written statement of terms and conditions given to employees, as required by the **Employment Protection (Consolidation) Act 1978**, and all amendments to these
- copies of any disciplinary warnings, etc issued to individual employees.

Q8.2 **What restrictions are placed on the information I keep concerning my employees?**

A.   If your records are kept manually (ie not on computer) there are currently no restrictions on the data kept by an employer.

If your personnel records are kept on computer, the information you keep and the use made of it is regulated by the **Data Protection Act 1984**. The Act requires, with few exceptions, that all data users register with the Data Protection Registrar. The main requirements concerning data are:

- data must be obtained and processed fairly and lawfully
- personal data must be kept for only one (or more) specified and lawful purpose(s)
- such data can only be held or disclosed in a manner compatible with the purpose(s) for which it is held
- data shall be adequate, relevant and not excessive.

Longer term, it is intended that all personal data, whether kept on computer or not, will have to meet the requirements listed above.

Q8.3   What rights do my employees have to see the information I keep about them?

A.   If the information is computer-based then, as described above, the **Data Protection Act 1984** provides them with the right to see it. This does not apply to manually created records although, in time, under European Union (EU) proposals, similar rights will be extended to manual data.

From the point of view of good management practice, however, it makes sense to make all records available to the staff concerned, remembering to respect the confidentiality of each employee.

Q8.4   What data would you advise me to keep to ensure that I do not fall foul of equal opportunities law?

A.   Equal opportunities legislation is designed to ensure that people are not discriminated against on grounds of sex or ethnic origin. An employer, particularly when recruiting, may be expected to show that he or she did not discriminate illegally against individuals. Employers are therefore advised to keep records of all applicants and reasons for not offering them employment, so that should someone bring an action against them on grounds of discrimination, evidence will be readily available showing that selection was made on grounds of competence and suitability for the job.

In the case of a large employer, it is recommended that sex and ethnic monitoring is conducted regularly throughout all levels of the organisation. Monitoring should show the composition of the workforce analysed by occupational groups, organisational levels, ethnic origin and sex.

The Commission for Racial Equality and the Equal Opportunities Commission advocate in codes of practice the elimination of discrimination through the development and operation of equal opportunities policies. They have powers to decide to carry out an investigation and this documentation is invaluable in such a case.

Q8.5   Am I obliged to give a reference concerning an ex-employee or one about to leave my employment?

A.   You are not obliged by law to give a reference concerning an employee or ex-employee, though obviously the vast majority of employers do give references. Assessing a new employee's competence for a job would be made much more difficult without this practice.

Q8.6   Can an ex-employee bring an action against me as a result of a reference I have written?

A.   When an employer gives a reference he or she should tell the truth. Truthful references will create few problems for the employer writing them although, in theory, an employee could sue for defamation if a reference contained an unprovable statement. References are covered by "qualified privilege" which means that an employer can be sued only if he or she acted "maliciously". It is very difficult to prove malice in a court of law and as there is no legal aid for defamation cases it is very unlikely that an employee will bring an action for defamation. Many employers limit such a risk by only giving oral references by telephone.

Q8.7 **Can employees see references I have received about them, or can past employees ask for details of references I have written about them?**

A.   It would appear that if the reference is kept on a computer then the employee will have a right of access to it under the **Data Protection Act 1984**. Otherwise, if the record is kept manually there is no automatic right to see a reference. However, should a dispute go to court then a reference may have to be produced to the court.

Q8.8 **Am I responsible to another employer as result of a reference I provide for him or her concerning an ex-employee of mine?**

A.   If in providing a reference to another employer you knowingly give false or misleading information, you may be liable for negligence. However, no such cases have been recorded recently. You may limit your liability by writing "without prejudice" across the top of a reference.

If employers deliberately provide false references or an employee forges or alters a reference they can be prosecuted in a magistrates' court under the **Servants' Character Act 1792**.

9. EMPLOYEE RELATIONS

Q9.1 **Am I obliged to have a means of consulting with staff on any matters concerning their employment?**

A. In the UK, as opposed to the situation in continental Europe, there are few regulations concerning the creation or operation of consultative arrangements between management and staff. The two important exceptions are concerned with redundancy and with safety.

1. *Redundancy.* An employer who recognises an independent trade union in respect of a group of employees must consult with that trade union if he or she plans to make any members of that union redundant. The following time limits apply:

    – 10–99 employees — at least 30 days before the first dismissals take effect

    – 100 or more employees — at least 90 days before the first dismissals take effect.

2. *Health and safety.* In the case of health and safety matters, the **Safety Representatives and Safety Committees Regulations 1977** require an employer to form a safety committee when so requested by two or more employees.

Q9.2 **We have a trade union in our organisation which represents a number of our employees. What information do I have to pass on to this trade union?**

A. The **Trade Union and Labour Relations (Consolidation) Act 1990** imposes a duty on employers who recognise trade unions for the purpose of collective bargaining to provide union representatives (when requested in writing) with information:

    – without which the representatives would be impeded in carrying on collective bargaining to a material extent, and

- which should be disclosed to them for the purpose of collective bargaining in accordance with good industrial relations practice.

Employers are not obliged to disclose the following:

- information against the national interest

- information which, if disclosed, would result in contravention of a prohibition or an enactment

- information acquired in confidence

- information about an individual unless he or she agrees to the disclosure

- information likely to damage the employer's business for reasons other than its effect on collective bargaining

- information obtained by the employer which is concerned with legal proceedings.

Q9.3 **Am I obliged to recognise and negotiate with a trade union which claims to have a significant number of my employees as members?**

A. Recognition of a trade union is entirely within the control of the employer. The employer can choose to recognise or not recognise a trade union. "Recognition" normally means that an employer is willing to negotiate with a union on some or all of the following matters:

- terms and conditions of employment and/or physical working conditions

- employment, termination or suspension of employment or the duties of one or more workers

- allocation of work between workers or groups of workers

- disciplinary matters

- membership or non-membership of a union by a worker

- facilities for union officials

- negotiation or consultation machinery.

Whether or not to recognise a union can be important because only recognised unions have the right to have certain information disclosed to them.

Q9.4   Can I refuse to employ someone because of his or her membership of a trade union?

A.   No. The **Trade Union and Labour Relations (Consolidation) Act 1992** makes it unlawful to refuse employment to someone on the grounds of union membership.

Q9.5   Can I refuse to employ someone because of his or her refusal to join a trade union?

A.   No. As written in the preceding answer, the **Trade Union and Labour Relations (Consolidation) Act 1992** makes it unlawful to refuse employment to someone on the grounds of union membership, ie because a person is or is not a member of a trade union, or because he or she is unwilling to join a trade union as a requirement of employment.

Q9.6   What rights to time off do union members have?

A.   Union officials have the right to paid time off from work in order to carry out trade union duties and undergo industrial relations training. Union members may be allowed to take part in union activities without pay.

Q9.7   Can I dismiss someone because they took part in trade union activities at a time inconvenient to the business?

A.   In essence, employees who take time off without permission are in breach of their employment contract and can be subject to appropriate disciplinary action. However, employees who are also union officials and who are members of a recognised union are allowed to take reasonable time off during working hours to take part in activities of that union or where the employee is representing that union. Any industrial action is excluded from this legislation so employees taking time off, for example, to strike, are technically in breach of contract and could be subject to disciplinary action and possibly dismissal.

Q9.8   Can I dismiss someone because they took part in industrial action, eg a strike?

A.   Employees who take time off without permission are in breach of their employment contract and can be subject to appropriate disciplinary action. Thus employees taking time off to strike are technically in breach of contract and could be subject to disciplinary action, possibly including dismissal depending on your disciplinary rules and past practice. However, all employees involved in the action must be treated in a similar way — otherwise there may be grounds for an action for unfair dismissal.

Q9.9   Can a trade union be sued for damages for inducing breaches of employment contracts?

A.   Unions used to benefit from a privileged position in that they could not be sued for liabilities arising from industrial action. However, union disputes benefit from immunity in civil law only if the dispute is between the employer and his or her employees and if a proper ballot of the members has been conducted. Secondary action is therefore not subject to any immunity and those concerned can be sued for damages. If unlawful action is authorised by a union, an injured party may sue the union for damages which can be as much as £250,000.

Q9.10   Does the "closed shop" still exist?

A.   No. A "closed shop" traditionally referred to an employer who had an agreement with a union that all employees (or certain categories of employee) would become members of the union. Effectively, recent employment legislation has made the "closed shop" inoperative, mainly because employers can no longer make employees join a union.

Q9.11 **As an employer, am I obliged to help a union to conduct a ballot on our premises?**

A.   An employer is obliged, so far as is reasonable, to allow his or her premises to be used for a union ballot by employees who are union members. This only applies where:

–   the employer and any associated employer employs more than 20 employees

–   the trade union is recognised by the employer for collective bargaining.

If an employer refuses, the union can present a complaint to an industrial tribunal.

10. TRANSFER OF UNDERTAKINGS

Q10.1 What is meant by a "transfer of undertakings"?

A. The **Transfer of Undertakings (Protection of Employment) Regulations 1981** (SI 1981 No. 1794) were designed to implement the EC Directive on Acquired Rights (77/187/EEC).

The regulations apply to changes of ownership of businesses which are effected by sale or other disposition or by operation by law. They cover the transfer of commercial undertakings and many types of public sector services from one person to another as long as it is the business itself which is being disposed of. Relevant transfers would include the sale of a business to a new owner, the merger of two companies or the integration of a subsidiary's activities within a parent company's business, providing that both the assets and the business are transferred. Transfers also cover the contracting out of activities such as catering, cleaning and pension fund administration by public sector authorities.

Q10.2 Are public sector organisations covered by the Transfer of Undertakings (Protection of Employment) Regulations 1981?

A. Yes. There was some doubt as to whether public sector operations would be classified as "commercial operations". However, operations such as local authority catering facilities, which are subject to compulsory competitive tendering, are within the scope of the regulations. Thus contractors who wished to tender for contracts offering less favourable terms and conditions must now take over all employees on completion of the transfer, on no less favourable terms and conditions. Not to do so enables employees made redundant to claim unfair dismissal from the transferring employer.

Q10.3 **What is the link between transfer of undertakings regulations and the Acquired Rights Directive?**

A. In 1994, there was a far-reaching decision by the European Court of Justice concerning the interpretation of the EC Acquired Rights Directive and its impact on the **Transfer of Undertakings (Protection of Employment) Regulations 1981** (TUPE). The case of *Schmidt v Spar- und Leihkasse der früheren Ämter Bordesholm, Kiel und Cronshagen* (1994) IRLR 302 concerned a woman who was employed by the bank as a cleaner and was dismissed when the cleaning was contracted out. It was decided that the decisive factor in determining if a transfer has taken place is whether the business retains its identity, in other words is the new employer resuming or continuing the same or similar activities? This interpretation did not have regard for the transfer of the assets of the business as stated in TUPE. This means that virtually all contracting-out operations will be regarded as transfers of business. Subsequent to the *Schmidt* ruling, the Court of Appeal has followed the ruling over the transfer of a contracted cleaning service in the health sector (*Dines v (1) Initial Health Care Services Ltd (2) Pall Mall Services Group Ltd* (1994) IRLR 336).

Q10.4 **If a catering contract changes hands, do the staff all have to be made redundant or could some be transferred?**

A. The staff would be automatically transferred. Regulation 5 of the **Transfer of Undertakings (Protection of Employment) Regulations 1981** states that "the contracts of employment of employees in the undertaking are automatically transferred from the transferor to transferee".

Q10.5 **By law, what information regarding my employees' pay and benefits do I have to provide to a prospective purchaser or contractor of the undertaking?**

A. There is no legal guidance available, however the following should be regarded as the minimum:

- names, job titles, start dates and current salary of all employees
- normal hours for all employees
- holiday and sickness entitlement for all employees
- information on membership of pension schemes
- detail of benefits in kind, including bonus schemes.

Q10.6 If I acquire staff, do I become liable for accrued benefits, etc?

A.   Yes. Employees receive continuity of employment. This means that all service with the transferring employer is deemed to be with the new employer. Occupational pension schemes are not covered by the necessity to have no less favourable terms.

Q10.7 Can an incoming contractor offer terms and conditions of service that are less favourable to the employees?

A.   No, to do so would entitle the employee to leave and claim constructive dismissal which would then be automatically unfair. Reorganisation for technical and economic reasons is potentially fair.

Q10.8 If not all relevant information was disclosed to me when I took over a contract, what action can I take?

A.   The only action is to sue the transferor through the courts. This will usually take the form of an incoming business or contractor suing the outgoing operator for giving inaccurate information about its current employees' terms and conditions, which results in miscalculations on the tender bid. At the time of writing, a number of such actions are being considered by the courts.

Q10.9 If an employee is dismissed as a result of a transfer, can that employee claim compensation for unfair dismissal?

A.   Yes, if the dismissal is as a result of the transfer, either immediately before or after the transfer takes place. To claim unfair dismissal the employees must have been employed continuously for 104 weeks, although this may be changed as a result of cases pending.

A tribunal is likely to regard dismissals at the time of the transfer as being for a transfer-related reason.

Q10.10 If employees who transfer are members of a recognised trade union, is that recognition also transferred?

A. Yes. Regulation 9 of the **Transfer of Undertaking (Protection of Employment) Regulations 1981** states that recognition will also be transferred, but only where the undertaking or part transferred retains an identity distinct from the remainder of the transferee's undertaking.

11. REDUNDANCY

Q11.1   **What is redundancy?**

A.   This is defined in s.81(2) of the **Employment Protection (Consolidation) Act 1978**. Essentially it will occur in one of the following circumstances:

- an entire business or particular work location closes down
- a job disappears or changes its content significantly
- there is a reduction in an employer's need for employees to carry out a particular type of work; this might be as a result of the amount of work to be done or a change in working practice.

Redundancy is about a job and not about the individual person doing it.

Q11.2   **What general guidance is there on the selection of employees for redundancy?**

A.   Redundancy selection procedures will be covered in a procedural agreement with workers' representatives, or an organisation may have a customary arrangement. However, an employer's selection criteria should be objective and should be capable of being verified by reference to data.

An employer will have to prove that criteria for redundancy are fair and have been objectively and equally applied to all employees concerned.

In the past, the concept of "last in first out" (LIFO) has been applied by many, but there have been challenges that this is indirectly discriminatory against women, who tend to have more job breaks than men.

ACAS has a code of practice for dealing with redundancy, and this should be reflected in an individual organisation's methods. If redundancies are to be expected then it is advisable to plan for this by allowing natural wastage and the recruitment of temporary employees so as to reduce the number of enforced redundancies. Safer criteria include opting for those over normal retirement age first, followed by those who wish to volunteer. Employers do not like to lose enthusiastic, skilled employees and so objective selection based on the skills and qualifications will be more suited to the needs of the business.

Criteria which are often used include attendance, age and fitness, ability, skills and experience, performance and length of service. Negative criteria such as a poor disciplinary record and absenteeism may also be used, but it is vital that decisions are based on facts and that the criteria used to judge all staff concerned are consistent. An employer will therefore have to show that there has been a comparative analysis of appropriate data relating to all relevant employees. All this indicates the need to have sound procedures in place and good records relating to discipline, absenteeism and work performance.

Dismissal for redundancy will be automatically unfair if the employee was selected for a reason relating to trade union membership. Redundancy owing to pregnancy would also be automatically unlawful.

Q11.3 Can I simply keep my better employees when deciding on redundancies?

A. You can if you apply objective criteria, and can demonstrate that you applied all the criteria equally to all affected employees.

Q11.4 What is a claim of unfair selection for redundancy?

A. This is essentially a claim of unfair dismissal in which the former employee is contesting the basis of his or her selection for redundancy.

Q11.5 How are redundancy payments calculated?

A. There are statutory payments, but an employer may have an agreement with its employees to enhance these payments.

Statutory payments are based on age and length of continuous service, and are as follows:

– one week's pay for each year of employment between the ages of 22 and 40

– one and a half weeks' pay for each year's service over the age of 41

– half a week's pay for each year's service between the ages of 18 and 21.

Employees who have reached their contractual retiring age are not entitled to a statutory redundancy payment, even if that age is less than 65. That age must be the same for male and female employees doing the same job. If it is not possible to establish a "customary" retiring age, 65 will be deemed to be the norm.

Q11.6 How do I calculate continuous employment?

A.   Simply work backwards from the effective date of termination and calculate the number of complete years of continuous service, excluding service under the age of 18. It is important that you include the time when female employees were away on approved maternity leave as this counts as continuous service. The statement of terms and conditions of employment should state the date on which continuous service commenced.

Q11.7 What is the basis of the calculation of an average weekly wage?

A.   An average weekly wage comprises two factors: the "normal" working hours and the average hourly rate. Normal hours are those stipulated in the conditions of employment. This would not normally include overtime unless it is a requirement of the employer that this overtime is always worked, and is therefore a condition of employment. Overtime hours can not be counted unless a fixed amount has been agreed which was obligatory on both sides. There have been a number of cases on this issue, where tribunals have allowed overtime to be calculated as part of the normal hours, but these have often been overturned by the Employment Appeal Tribunal (EAT) or the Court of Appeal (*Tarmac Roadstone Holdings v Peacock* (1973) ICR 273).

Where there is no normal working week, this is calculated as the average number of hours worked over the 12 weeks prior to the calculation date.

The maximum amount that can be calculated for a week's pay for redundancy purposes, and also for payments for unfair dismissal, is set by the Secretary of State for Employment. It is currently £210 per week.

Q11.8 Can part-time workers receive redundancy payments?

A.   Yes. Employees aged 18 or over but under 65 who have worked for an employer continuously for 104 weeks now qualify.

Q11.9 Would an employee currently on maternity leave qualify for a redundancy payment?

A.   Yes. Staff on maternity leave are regarded as employees if they have stated their right to return to work after the appropriate period of time. This again indicates the need for good employee records, including those who may not currently be at your workplace. Similarly such employees should not be forgotten when looking for suitable alternative employment for potentially redundant employees.

Q11.10 What are my obligations concerning consultation with the workforce regarding redundancy?

A.   In most cases, an employer who fails to consult with employees is going to be found to have unfairly dismissed them. This became clear in a judgment from the House of Lords in *Polkey v A E Dayton Services Ltd* (1987) IRLB 503: "...in the case of redundancy, the employer will normally not act reasonably unless he warns and consults any employees affected or their representatives, adopts a fair basis on which to select for redundancy and takes such steps as may be reasonable to avoid or minimise redundancy by redeployment within his own organisation."

Notice of dismissal should not be issued until consultation has taken place. The consultation should include the following explanations:

- the need for redundancies
- why particular employees have been identified as candidates for redundancy
- the marking system under any selection criteria
- why the employer has not been able to offer alternative work.

Other areas of consultation include:

- possible ways to avoid the redundancies
- possible methods of reducing the numbers to be made redundant
- methods of mitigating the consequences of the redundancies.

The employees should be allowed to make comments on any of the points and these should be considered by the employer.

If an organisation recognises a trade union which represents the category of employees who are being dismissed, there are some statutory time-limits set out regarding consultation:

(a) where the employer is proposing to dismiss as redundant 100 or more employees at one establishment within a period of 90 days or less, at least 90 days' notice should be given before the first of those dismissals takes effect, or

(b) where the employer is proposing to dismiss as redundant 20 or more employees at one establishment within a period of 90 days or less, consultation must be made in good time and in any event at least 30 days' notice should be given before the first of those dismissals takes effect.

This requirement has been extended to include consultation with employees for whom there is no recognised trade union at the workplace (the **Collective Redundancies and Transfer of Undertakings (Protection of Employment) (Amendment) Regulations 1995**, coming into force in March 1996). In this case, the consultation would take place with the "appropriate representatives". This is anyone elected by the employees to represent their views. This new requirement, therefore, provides for consultation with all affected workers.

Q11.11 Do I have to offer alternative employment to a redundant employee if it is available?

A.   Yes. Employers have an obligation to see what alternative vacancies exist, not only in their own company but also in associated companies. Failure to do so may make the redundancy unfair dismissal. Also, it should not be assumed that an employee is not prepared to work for less money or on shorter hours. It is good practice to circulate vacancies to redundant employees and then invite applications. If employers do not look for alternative employment or make assumptions about what jobs employees may accept, and therefore do not offer vacancies to them, there could be a justifiable case for unfair dismissal (*Nationwide Anglia Building Society v Hooper* EAT 360/91).

Q11.12 Can an employee refuse to accept alternative employment, and would this affect his or her rights to a redundancy payment?

A.   An employee can reject alternative employment if he or she feels that the alternative employment is unreasonable. Section 82(5) of the **Employment Protection (Consolidation) Act 1978** provides that "if the employee unreasonably refuses a suitable offer of employment, he is not entitled to a redundancy payment." The question of reasonableness is one that can often only be decided by a tribunal.

Q11.13 **Do I have to give employees who may be made redundant time off for job seeking and training?**

A.   Yes. Section 31 of the **Employment Protection (Consolidation) Act 1978** states that employees who have been given notice of dismissal by reason of redundancy are entitled to "reasonable paid time off during working hours for the purpose of looking for new employment or to make arrangements for training." Many employers set up job-hunting facilities on their premises if they have to make a large number of redundancies.

Q11.14 **What can be done to minimise the impact of redundancy on employees?**

A.   Redundancy can be a traumatic experience for employees, and they should receive as much support as possible. Help can take the form of counselling, particularly on financial matters. Employees may also benefit from help with job-hunting and the preparation of CVs. In addition, employees can receive training on how to present themselves in a job interview. Such additional help to employees, under notice of redundancy, is often referred to as "outplacement".

Q11.15 **How long can employees "try out" a new job within the company without losing their rights to redundancy pay?**

A.   Employees are allowed a trial period of up to four weeks to enable them to assess whether alternative employment is suitable and acceptable to them. Section 82 of the **Employment Protection (Consolidation) Act 1978** provides that "an employee who unreasonably terminates or gives notice to terminate a new contract of suitable employment during the trial period loses the right to a payment."

12. DISCIPLINE

Q12.1 **What are my legal obligations regarding the disciplining and dismissal of employees?**

A.   ACAS has produced a code of practice relating to disciplinary procedures. Whilst this is only advisory, it is good practice to follow these guidelines and incorporate them into your own organisation's disciplinary procedures. In an industrial tribunal, an employer would be expected to be familiar with the code. Essentially you should give an employee a oral warning (dependent on the nature of the problem), followed by a written warning and then a final written warning.

     If you dismiss an employee, he or she is entitled to receive a written reason for the dismissal if he or she requests it. It is important to remember that this document could subsequently be used in any tribunal hearings.

Q12.2 **What must I do to ensure that employees are aware of company rules, etc?**

A.   Knowledge of company rules is vital for all employees, but especially new ones, who will be unaware of what general rules apply within an organisation. A new employee could unwittingly break a rule within a few hours or days of starting a job unless rules are explained. This is especially true in the catering industry, where employers have different rules about, for example, eating and drinking on duty. The issue of employees taking home waste food is another potential problem for the employer. All rules must be stated clearly and applied consistently. The time of the employees' induction is an obvious time for this. Those organisations that operate some form of employee induction record card, perhaps with employees' signatures indicating that they have had the rules explained to them, will find it useful.

The induction period should also be used to explain the organisation's disciplinary procedures. It should be noted that a failure to follow the laid down procedure could lead to a dismissal being found to be unfair, in spite of what may appear to be valid grounds.

Q12.3 If employees are not performing satisfactorily, what must I do to improve the situation before taking disciplinary action?

A. A disciplinary procedure is not simply a series of stages leading to a dismissal. Its aims are also to encourage employees to improve their performance or stop breaking rules. However, if an employee's performance is not up to standard, the employer should take steps to improve it, for example by giving further training or instruction.

It is good practice to record such training in the event of there being a need for formal disciplinary procedures at a later date.

Q12.4 Do employees have a right of representation during disciplinary procedures?

A. Yes. The ACAS code of practice on disciplinary procedures suggests that employees have a right of representation, and this should be written into an organisation's disciplinary procedures, which should include a right of appeal. In some cases employers suggest that a person to be disciplined is accompanied by a colleague or a friend. In the initial stages this should be an employee of the company or a recognised trade union representative. It may be advisable that the friend is of the same sex as the person to be disciplined. It is also good practice for the employer to have a witness present in such interviews.

Q12.5 In what circumstances might it be appropriate to suspend an employee?

A. Where it is not possible to investigate a case fully at the time, suspension may be a suitable option. This allows the pressure of the "heat of the moment" to pass, so that there is a better chance of a cool, rational decision being taken. It also allows time to talk to other staff who may be able to contribute to the investigation. Sometimes those with the authority to conduct disciplinary interviews may not be present so, again, suspension would be appropriate. The right to suspend employees should be written into the disciplinary procedures of the organisation.

Q12.6 How long can a warning stay in place?

A. This will depend on the seriousness of the problem and what has been written into an organisation's disciplinary procedures. However, when taking disciplinary action, it is important to confirm to employees in writing what is expected of them, and this may well include a statement relating to the monitoring of behaviour over a set period of time (eg timekeeping over the next three months). If an employee has been well behaved for a long period of time and then "re-offended", you may have to start the formal disciplinary procedure again, with the employee having a "clean slate" in relation to previous written warnings.

Q12.7 If I have a disciplinary procedure, do I have to follow it even for very serious cases of misconduct?

A. Yes. Your disciplinary rules and procedures should cover misconduct and gross misconduct.

Whilst a capability problem may require you to give employees some time to improve, in the case of misconduct the employee may be expected to resolve the problem immediately by changing his or her behaviour.

In the case of gross misconduct, the rules should specify, among other things, what action the employer can take. This may include suspension, with or without pay, or instant dismissal without accrued holiday pay.

Q12.8 **If two employees are known to be involved in a personal relationship, what rights does an employer have concerning this situation?**

A. Some organisations have a policy on personal relationships between employees. If this is the case then it must be made clear at the start of employment exactly what the policy is, the action those concerned must take and the likely outcome in terms of action, if any, by the employer. Of major importance is the impact or likely impact that the relationship will have on the ability of the employees to perform their duties.

Q12.9 **Do I need to use the disciplinary procedures with a new employee or can I simply terminate the employment?**

A. The first four weeks of employment are effectively regarded as a trial period and no notice period is required during this time **(Employment Protection (Consolidation) Act 1978** (EP(C)A)). Thereafter one week's notice is required per year of service. Express terms in the main statement of terms and conditions of employment may override this by providing an extended probationary period and making provision for more generous periods of notice. Many employers would apply the same disciplinary code to all employees whether new or long serving.

It must be remembered that it is also stated within the EP(C)A that it is automatically unfair to dismiss employees on the grounds of pregnancy and trade union membership.

13. DISMISSAL

Q13.1 What are the "fair" reasons for dismissal?

A. The right not to be unfairly dismissed was first granted under the **Industrial Relations Act 1971**. Following a series of amendments and re-enactments, it is now consolidated into the provisions of the **Trade Union and Labour Relations (Consolidation) Act 1992**.

It is important to distinguish between wrongful and unfair dismissal, the former being concerned with a common law offence of breach of contract. The legislation confers the right not to be dismissed unfairly, provided that the employee has been employed for the required period of time (in most, but not all, cases two years) and is not older than the relevant age.

The fair reasons for dismissal under s.57(1) of the **Industrial Relations Act 1971** are as follows.

1. *Capability:* a reason related to the capability or qualifications of the employee performing the work of the kind which he or she was employed by the employer to do. "Capability" is assessed by reference to skill, aptitude, health or any other physical or mental ability. "Qualifications" means any degree, diploma or other academic, technical or professional qualification relevant to the position which the employee holds.

2. *Misconduct:* a reason related to the conduct of the employee.

3. *Redundancy:* the employee was made redundant. Details of redundancy are dealt with in chapter 11.

4. *Contravention of Enactment:* the employee could not continue to work in the position that he or she held without contravention (either on his or her part or that of the employer) of a duty or restriction imposed by or under an enactment.

5. *Some other substantial reason* of a kind to justify dismissal.

Section 61 of the Act stipulates that employees who are replacements for employees who are absent through pregnancy or maternity leave can be dismissed fairly on the employees' return. Other examples of fair dismissal include the expiry of a fixed-term contract and the frustration of a contract through the imprisonment of an employee. However, each case would have to be considered on its own merits.

The onus is on the employer to prove the reason(s) for dismissal and if unable to prove that the reason was one of those mentioned above, the dismissal will be unfair. It is important that the employer is seen to act reasonably at all times. This requires that he or she has made known to the employees all house and disciplinary rules (see Q12.2). Also, the employer should provide training for employees who are performing poorly and give them an opportunity to improve their performance. In addition, it is important that the employer acts fairly with all employees and is consistent in dealing with breaches of discipline.

Q13.2 **What is the difference between "wrongful" and "unfair" dismissal?**

A.   Very simply, wrongful dismissal is where an employer dismisses someone and the dismissal is in breach of the contract of employment. The remedy for wrongful dismissal is to bring a civil action for breach of contract in the county court or the High Court. An action for such a breach of contract can be brought at any time including where an offer of employment has been made and accepted but subsequently withdrawn by the employers before employment has commenced. This action is rarely undertaken owing to the costs involved.

Unfair dismissal arises under the **Employment Protection (Consolidation) Act 1978** (EP(C)A). The EP(C)A lays down five fair reasons for dismissal. Dismissal for reasons other than these may constitute unfair dismissal. Actions for unfair dismissal are brought before an industrial tribunal. Costs of an action before an industrial tribunal can be very modest whereas an action for wrongful dismissal in a county court will invariably involve expensive legal fees.

Protection from unfair dismisal arises in the main after two years' service (although currently under review) whereas action for wrongful dismissal can be instituted at any time.

Q13.3   Which employees are protected against unfair dismissal?

A.   Protected employees are those who have worked for an employer continuously for at least 104 weeks. Until the **Employment Protection (Part-time Employees) Regulations 1995** (SI 1995 No. 31) were enacted, the rights were applicable only to those working an average of 16 hours per week or more or for more than 8 hours per week after 5 years' continuous service. Now, part-timers also qualify for protection from unfair dismissal. At the time of writing, it is being argued that the two year qualifying period is also discriminatory, as many women take employment for periods shorter than this and hence receive no protection from unfair dismissal.

Q13.4   What is the basis for the calculation of compensation in a case of unfair dismissal?

A.   Generally, there are three possible remedies in the case of unfair dismissal: reinstatement of the employee, re-engagement or an award of compensation.

Compensation can consist of a basic award, a compensatory award and, in cases where the tribunal requires reinstatement or re-engagement and the employer refuses, an additional award. There may also be a special award for dismissals relating to trade union and health and safety reasons.

1.   *Basic award:* the basic award is calculated as for redundancy pay:

- one week's pay for each year of employment between the ages of 22 and 40

- one and a half weeks' pay for each year's service if the employee is over the age of 41

- half a week's pay for each year's service between the ages of 18 and 21 inclusive.

The Government sets the maximum weekly pay that is used to calculate benefits, and there is a maximum length of service of 20 years for calculation purposes. If the dismissal took place after an employee's 64th birthday, the compensation would be reduced by 12 equal parts for each month over the age of 64, thus having no award as soon as the age of 65 is reached.

To establish continuous service, the employer should determine the effective date of termination of the employment, and then count backwards the number of completed years of service, subject to a maximum of 20. The maximum calculable weekly wage is currently £210, hence the maximum basic award would be £6300 (20 × 1.5 × 210).

2.   *Compensatory award:* this is the sum that the tribunal feels is just and equitable, taking account of any losses suffered by the employee as a result of the dismissal, in so far as any loss that is deemed the fault of the employer. This loss would include any expenses reasonably incurred by the employee as a consequence of the dismissal, and loss of any benefit which might reasonably be expected had the dismissal not taken place.

Currently, the amount of a compensatory award may not exceed £17,600. However, there is the possibility of unlimited compensation in race discrimination cases if the employer fails to offer reinstatement. The tribunal will consider normal benefits, such as the value of a company car, when making its calculations. The employee has the normal common law obligation, which is to mitigate the losses involved.

3. *Additional award:* this could be awarded by the tribunal when an order of reinstatement or re-engagement is not complied with. If the reason for dismissal was for unlawful sex or race discrimination, the award will be between 26 and 52 weeks' salary. In other cases it will be between 13 and 26 weeks' salary.

4. *Special awards:* in the case of union-related dismissals under ss.152 or 153 of the **Trade Union and Labour Relations (Consolidation) Act 1992**, or certain health and safety dismissals, a special award may be made by the tribunal except in cases where the complainant does not seek reinstatement or re-engagement. Such awards will not be made if the employee has unreasonably refused an offer of suitable alternative employment.

   The special award is calculated as the greater of £13,400 or 104 weeks' pay, with a maximum of £26,800. If the tribunal makes an order of reinstatement or re-engagement and this is not complied with, the compensation is increased to the greater sum of £20,100 or 156 weeks' pay (no ceiling).

Q13.5 What is meant by constructive dismissal?

A. In a case of constructive dismissal, there is no formal dismissal of the employee by the employer, but instead the employee is forced to resign through the employer's unreasonable behaviour.

Each individual case would, of course, have to be looked at on its merits, but the **Employment Protection (Consolidation) Act 1978** attempts to protect employees in such a situation. There would normally have to be a fundamental breach of the contract by the employer for it to be seen as constructive dismissal. Often contracts are not written down, and therefore a breach of contract can be difficult to prove. It is for the employee to prove that he or she has been dismissed and, in the case of constructive dismissal, he or she must prove the term which is being relied upon in order to show that there has been a breach of contract by the employer.

Q13.6 If an employee has been guilty of misconduct for some time, am I allowed to dismiss the employee?

A. You are, but you may not be able to dismiss the employee as quickly as you would like. If you have been overlooking some malpractice, even though it is listed in disciplinary rules, then it may be difficult to defend the dismissal. What you must do is to restate the rules and the disciplinary procedures, perhaps via a staff meeting or a note to all employees, and then be consistent in enforcing the rules with all employees. Once it has then been re-established that such behaviour is not acceptable, disciplinary action may be needed. It should be remembered, however, that you should follow your disciplinary procedure as suggested by the ACAS code of practice.

Q13.7 Can I withhold pay for employees found guilty of misconduct?

A. No. Employees have carried out their part of a contract by supplying their labour, and therefore should be paid for it. The house rules, however, may allow for employees to be dismissed without receiving paid notice or accrued holiday pay in cases of gross misconduct. Employees should be made aware of this in the employer's disciplinary rules.

Q13.8 Can I dismiss someone because of their behaviour outside the workplace?

A. Yes, in certain circumstances, particularly where someone is convicted of a criminal offence. However, there are many factors to take into account as mere conviction is not enough. The nature and severity of the offence, as well as the position occupied by the person concerned, may have to be considered, as could the views of other employees and even customers and clients (*Nottingham-shire County Council v Bowly* (1978) IRLR 252).

Q13.9   Can I dismiss any employee for persistent, genuine illness?

A.   Yes, as this could be justified on the grounds of incapability (see Q13.1). However, such cases need to be handled very carefully. The Employment Appeal Tribunal (EAT) has suggested that the following factors should be taken into account when considering such cases:

- length of service
- length of future potential employment
- nature of the job
- length and effect of the illness
- need for the work to be done
- risk of acquiring obligations to a replacement employee
- whether wages are still being paid
- acts and statements of the employee
- whether a reasonable employer could be expected to wait any longer
- contractual provision for sick pay
- prospects of recovery.

Q13.10 What is the difference between dismissal and summary dismissal?

A.   A summary dismissal is a dismissal without giving the contractually required notice, ie instant dismissal. This would normally apply for very serious misconduct and should be specified in the organisation's rules. Theft or violent behaviour often fall into this category. Nevertheless, it is important that such behaviour is fully investigated and that the employee is given an opportunity to fully state his or her case before any action is taken.

Employers should also consider stating their right to suspend employees pending investigation in such serious cases.

Q13.11 In what types of case will dismissal be automatically unlawful?

A.   In general, any cases that involve any form of race or sex discrimination will be unlawful. Dismissal on the grounds of belonging to, or participating in the activities of, a trade union would also be unlawful as would dismissal on any grounds associated with a transfer of undertakings. Dismissal on grounds related to an employee's pregnancy would also be automatically unlawful **(Trade Union and Labour Relations (Consolidation) Act 1992, s.152)**.

Q13.12 If I dismiss an employee for theft at work, and he or she is subsequently found not guilty in a criminal court, do I have to take the employee back?

A.   No. Any tribunal would simply consider the reasonableness of your actions in the light of information that you had to hand at the time of your dismissal. You would be expected, of course, to have carried out a full investigation, listening to the employee's views, before taking your action to dismiss.

14. TERMINATING CONTRACTS

See also chapters on *Dismissal* and *Discipline*.

Q14.1 How can I terminate a contract of employment?

A. Any fixed-term contracts come to an end when that time has lapsed, so a 10 day contract with an employee to work over a hotel's Christmas holiday programme terminates at the end of the 10 day period.

   If a contract does not contain terms concerning termination, it is usually terminated by mutual agreement. If the reason for termination is to do with the employee's performance or behaviour, this will come under the scope of unfair dismissal legislation contained in the **Employment Protection (Consolidation) Act 1978** as amended by the **Employment Act 1980** and **1982**. This specifies five fair reasons for dismissal — see Q13.1.

   In the case of gross misconduct the injured party, ie the employer, may consider the contract to be at an immediate end, without the need to give notice or money in lieu of notice.

Q14.2 Can I restrict who my employees work for after they leave my employment?

A. Many employers are concerned that a key employee, such as a sales manager, a chef or head waiter will compete with them should they leave. Employers therefore write restrictive covenants into employment contracts, the effect of which is to restrict the type of employment and/or geographical area in which an ex-employee can work for a specified period of time. For such a restrictive covenant to be upheld it will have to be shown that some specific interest is being protected, such as trade secrets or customers' names. Such actions carried out merely to prevent competition from the former employee will not be upheld (*Office Angels Ltd v Rainer-Thomas & O'Connor* (1991) IRLR 124).

Q14.3   Can an employee resign without giving notice?

A.   In normal circumstances, an employment contract can be termi-
         nated by the employee by resigning within the terms of the con-
         tract. Should an employee resign without giving proper notice and
         in circumstances which are not in response to a repudiatory breach
         by the employer, the employee is in breach of contract and, strictly
         speaking, could be sued for damages.

         However, where an employer has taken steps which are per-
         ceived by the employee to be a breach of contract (express or
         implied) the employee may resign without giving notice, possibly
         claiming constructive dismissal. Furthermore, dependent upon the
         circumstances, there may be grounds for bringing an action for
         unfair dismissal or even wrongful dismissal.

Q14.4   Can I dismiss staff without notice?

A.   Yes, if your statement of terms and conditions or your disciplinary
         rules say you can, for example in the case of gross misconduct.
         However, a full investigation would have to be carried out before
         such action occurred (see Q13.10).

Q14.5   Can an employer withdraw notice once it has been given?

A.   Notice of dismissal, once given, cannot be unilaterally withdrawn
         by the employer unless the employee agrees.

**Q14.6   Can an employee withdraw his or her notice once it has been
         given?**

A.   In the same way that notice of dismissal cannot be unilaterally
         withdrawn by the employer, a resignation also cannot be with-
         drawn, once given, unless the employer agrees. The exception to
         this rule is where an employee gives notice in the heat of the
         moment. Employers are advised not to accept a resignation given
         in the heat of the moment without some cooling-off period, as this
         could possibly be construed as constructive dismissal.

Q14.7   Can a contract be terminated by events outside the control of the two parties to the contract?

A.   Yes, in some circumstances. Where, owing to no fault of either party to the contract, the contract becomes impossible to perform or, if performed it would result in something radically different from what was originally intended when the contract was entered into, the contract is "frustrated". Effectively, in the employment field, if a contract is frustrated it will have been terminated without a dismissal or resignation. This principle is explained by the following Industrial Relations Court decision.

> A contract should cease to bind the parties if through no fault of either of them, unprovided for circumstances arise in which a contractual obligation becomes impossible of performance or in which performance of the obligation would be rendered a thing radically different from that which was undertaken by the contract.
>
> (*Marshall v Harland and Wolff Ltd* (1972) IRLR)

This doctrine has been applied in the case of an employee's permanent incapacity to work. In such a case, no dismissal takes place so the employee has no remedy for unfair dismissal.

The concept of frustration can also apply to an employee who is imprisoned (*FC Shepherd & Co Ltd v Jerrom* (1986) IRLR 358).

15. INDUSTRIAL TRIBUNALS

Q15.1   What is the scope of cases covered by an industrial tribunal?

A.   Industrial tribunals have historically dealt with statutory employment matters such as unfair dismissal, discrimination in employment, equal pay, Wages Act claims and statutory issues relating to trade unions. In addition, tribunals now have powers to deal with some contractual matters, which in the past would have been dealt with by the county court.

Q15.2   I have been called to attend an industrial tribunal as a result of a claim from a former employee. What processes are involved in this?

A.   1.   An industrial tribunal case is commenced by the ex-employee ("applicant") presenting an application to the Central Office of Industrial Tribunals. This is often done on an IT1 application form which details the basis of the claim.

2.   The employer ("respondent") will receive a copy of the application form and has 14 days in which to respond. It is possible to request a time extension and the tribunal will decide if this is possible. It may be that you require further information to carry out your investigation, and you can ask for "further and better particulars" from the other party.

3.   There may be a pre-hearing review, and if the tribunal feels that the applicant or the employer has little chance of success it can ask for a deposit of up to £150 to be paid. This is intended to discourage unnecessary claims and tribunal hearings. The tribunal may decide to undertake this review or it could be done at the request of one of the parties. Witnesses will not be called at such a review.

4.   The tribunal hearing is a public hearing and usually consists of three people, although the chairperson may sit alone. In

the case of unfair dismissal where the dismissal is admitted and the employee qualifies to make a claim, the employer will then take on the burden of proof to show that the dismissal was fair. The employer will briefly outline the case and will introduce witnesses and appropriate documentary evidence, such as written warnings, copies of house rules and statements of terms and conditions, etc. The members of the panel have the right to examine and cross-examine each witness. When all the witnesses have been called, there is a right to make a closing statement. The tribunal will then make a decision. The reasons for the decision are usually given in summary form, but extended reasons can be requested within 21 days of receipt of the summary reasons.

5.   Both parties have the right to appeal against a decision on a point of law to the Employment Appeals Tribunal (EAT) within 42 days of receipt of the extended reasons for the tribunal decision. There is no appeal against a finding of fact.

The **Industrial Tribunals (Constitution and Rules Procedure) Regulations 1993** were introduced as a result of the **Trade Union Reform and Employment Rights Act 1993** (TURERA).

Q15.3   What remedies can an industrial tribunal take if an employee's claim is proven?

A.   It will usually award compensation, but can also make an order to reinstate or re-engage the employee. If such an order is refused, then the employer may have to pay an additional award. If the tribunal considers that the employee is partially responsible for his or her dismissal because of his or her own conduct, the award may be adjusted accordingly.

Q15.4   Can any general contractual matters be brought before a tribunal or would some matters go to a county court?

A.   The **Industrial Tribunals Extensions of Jurisdiction (England and Wales) Order 1994** (SI 1994 No. 1623) and the **Industrial**

Tribunals Extensions of Jurisdiction (Scotland) Order 1994 (SI 1994 No. 1624) enable employees to bring contractual claims, which previously would have been heard in a county court, to a tribunal, where the subject of the claim arises from the termination of employment. This enables employees to claim for sums due to them on the termination of their employment, or regarding any issue which arises or is outstanding on the termination of employment, without all the cost involved in a county court hearing. No minimum period of employment is required to make such a claim and the tribunal has the power to award damages of up to £25,000. An employee may choose which jurisdiction to use.

Q15.5 **If an employee pursues a case in a tribunal, what documentation might the employer need, and would any official documentation be required?**

A.   As stated above, evidence to support the employer's case, such as the contract of employment, written warnings, records of disciplinary hearings and appeals, copies of your disciplinary procedures, terms and conditions of employment, house rules, evidence of training and evidence of absences, etc may all be relevant, depending on the nature of the claim.

Q15.6 **Is it possible to settle claims without the case going to tribunal?**

A.   Yes. However it is vital that this is not simply done as an *ex gratia* payment, but is carried out under the supervision of an official from ACAS.

Q15.7 **Do I need a lawyer to act on my behalf in a tribunal?**

A.   Not usually. Tribunal procedures have been made simple to allow employees and employers to present their own cases. However, if there are complicated legal concepts involved, then it is advisable to take legal advice, and possibly representation.

Q15.8   Is it possible to appeal against tribunal decisions?

A.   Yes, but only on a point of law. This would be made to the Employment Appeal Tribunal (EAT).

GLOSSARY

ACAS
The Advisory, Conciliation and Arbitration Service — the state agency responsible for advising on matters relating to employment, particularly when there are disputes between employers and employees and/or trade unions.

AVCs
Additional voluntary contributions (relating to pensions) — a system for purchasing additional pension benefits.

Children
People under school leaving age, as defined by law (see *Croner's Catering*, 4-20).

Common Law
Law made as a result of judges' decisions which become legal precedents for similar cases.

Constructive Dismissal
This may occur when an employee resigns because an employer has acted in a way (eg by imposing new conditions of work) which the employee perceives as a breach of contract on the part of the employer.

CV
Curriculum vitae — the latin expression for a person's personal history.

Direct Discrimination
This is treating a person less favourably because of his or her race or gender (see *Croner's Catering*, page 4-11).

EAT
Employment Appeal Tribunal — the "court" which hears appeals from Industrial Tribunals.

EC
European Commission — the "civil service" of the European Union.

EOC
Equal Opportunities Commission — the agency concerned with creating equal opportunities in the workplace.

GOQ
Genuine occupational qualification — in the discrimination context a GOQ is a requirement, characteristic or

qualification, in a personnel specification or job description, considered to be genuine and not specified in order to discriminate against particular groups of people.

HSE　　Health and Safety Executive — the agency concerned with health and safety at work issues. Some of its work is delegated to other authorities such as local authority environmental health departments.

Indirect　This is applying a requirement or condition which makes
Discrimination it more difficult for a particular group of people to satisfy than people not of that group.

IT　　Industrial Tribunal — the "court" concerned with resolving disputes occurring at the workplace, usually to provide an informal and speedy method for employees to enforce their rights against an employer.

MA　　Maternity Allowance — this is payable to women not entitled to Statutory Maternity Pay such as those with less than 26 weeks of continuous service with the same employer.

NICs　National Insurance Contributions — contributions deducted from employees and/or paid by employers towards the state National Insurance system.

PAYE　Pay As You Earn — the system of tax deductions from employees' earnings.

RSI　　Repetitive strain injury — a form of injury arising as a result of work tasks involving repeated movements over a period of time.

Safety　A worker who is elected or appointed to represent other
Representative workers on matters relating to safety at work. He or she may be elected or appointed by a recognised trade union.

SI

Statutory Instrument — secondary legislation which details legal requirements such as the **Employment (Part-time Employees) Regulations 1995** (SI 1995 No. 31).

SMP

Statutory Maternity Pay — pay to which women are entitled before and after giving birth to a child.

Spent Conviction

A conviction which may be treated by the offender as though it had never occurred because sufficient time has elapsed since it was imposed (see **Rehabilitation of Offenders Act 1974**, *Croner's Catering*, page 4-17). The consequence is that an applicant need not refer to it and an employer cannot act upon it (with some exceptions).

SSP

Statutory Sick Pay — pay to which a worker may be entitled as a result of absence through illness.

Statute Law

Law made by Parliament — much "Parliament-made" law is actually imposed through secondary legislation such as regulations.

TUPE

Transfer of Undertakings (Protection of Employment) Regulations 1981 — designed to provide employees with protection of employment (particularly continuity of service) upon change of ownership of the employing business.

Vicarious Liability

The liability of an employer for acts committed by his or her employees in the course of their work (see *Croner's Catering*, page 6-85).

WP1

A work permit issued by the Home Office for those workers requiring a work permit, eg non-EU nationals.

Young Persons

Those people over school leaving age, as defined by law, but still under 18 years of age.

INDEX

A

Access to Medical Reports Act 1988 48

Acquired Rights Directive 81, 82

additional award 100

additional voluntary contributions 39, 111

advertising 4

age limits 9, 10–11, 113

agency staff 17

AIDS 65–6

alternative employment 90

appeals 110

   see also Employment Appeal Tribunal

application forms 1–2

Article 8 of European Convention on Human Rights 65

Article 48 of Treaty of Rome 11

AVCs *see* additional voluntary contributions

Avon County Council v Howlett (1983) 33

B

ballots 80

basic award 98–9

behaving reasonably 13

behaviour outside workplace 101–2

Bellhaven Brewery Co. Ltd v McClean (1975) 59

benefits *see* pay

Bland v Stockport Borough Council (1993) 69

board and lodging 32

Burdett-Coutts and others v Hertfordshire County Council (1984) 27

business integration test 15–16

C

Cantor Fitzgerald (UK) Ltd v Wallace (1992) 22

capability 96

Capper Pass Ltd v Allan (1980) 37

care, duty of 14

casual workers 18, 20, 41

certificate of pregnancy (Mat B1) 51, 55

Child Support Agency 34

claims settlement 109

"closed shop" 79

Coleman v Skyrail Oceanic Ltd (1981) 7

Collier v Sunday Referee Publishing Co. Ltd (1940) 12

Commission for Racial Equality 74
company rules 92–3
compensation 83–4, 98–100
competence 14
Consumer Protection Act 1987 43
continuous employment
calculation 87
contractor, incoming 83
contracts 12–29
agency staff 17
casual workers 18
common law 20–1
conditions 26–7
dress code 22–3
employment agencies 29
full-time employees 17–18
general duties 12–15
imposing or implying terms 29
incorporation of other
documents 26
misrepresentation 28
negotiation of conditions 21–2
part-time workers 17–18
qualifying continuous service
for employees' rights 19
references 28–9
specifications 23–5
subcontractors 15–16
written statement 20–1
see also terminating
contravention of enactment 96
Control of Substances Hazardous
to Health Regulations 1988 64

control test 15
Cooner v PS Doal & Son (1988)
30
Copyright Act 1956 14
criminal offence 4, 101

D

data 72–4
Data Protection Act 1984 72, 73,
75
Delaney v Staples (1992) 30
Department for Education and
Employment 11, 36, 39
*Dines v (1) Initial Health Care
Services Ltd (2) Pall Mall
Services Group Ltd* (1994) 82
Disability Discrimination Act 1995
9
disabled persons 9–10
Disabled Persons (Employment)
Act 1944 and 1958 9
discipline 92–5
*Discount Tobacco & Confectionery
Ltd v Williamson* (1993) 34
discrimination 5, 7, 111, 112
see also race; sex
dismissal 78–9, 89, 94, 96–103
behaviour outside workplace
101–2
compensation 98–100
constructive 100–1, 111
fair reasons 96–7

illness, persistent genuine 102
misconduct 101
summary 102–3
theft at work 103
unfair 88–9, 97–100
unlawful 103
withholding pay 101
wrongful 97–8
domestic problems 6–7
dress code 22–3
Dryden v Greater Glasgow Health Board (1992) 68–9
duties 12–15

E

Eagland v British Telecommunications plc (1992) 38
EAT *see* Employment Appeal Tribunal
EHOs *see* environmental health officers
employee relations 76–80
Employment Act 1980 51, 104
Employment Act 1982 104
Employment Act 1989 10, 23
employment agencies 17, 29
Employment Appeal Tribunal 22–3, 70, 108, 110, 111
Employment Protection (Consolidation) Act 1978 30, 47, 72, 100, 104

contracts 15, 17, 20, 21, 23, 27, 29
dismissal 97, 100
redundancy 85, 90, 91
Employment Protection (Part-time Employees) Regulations 1995 17, 41–2, 98
environmental health officers 59, 63, 66
Equal Opportunities Commission 74, 112
equal opportunities law 73–4
Equal Pay Act 1970 37, 38
European Court of Justice 41, 42, 66, 82
European Union 11, 73

F

FC Shepherd & Co Ltd v Jerrom (1986) 106
Fire Precautions Act 1971 58
first aid cover 64–5
Food Handlers' Declaration 66
Food Safety Act 1990 23
Food Safety (General Food Hygiene) Regulations 1995 65
form IT1 107
form P9D 40, 44
form P11 44, 55
form P11D 40, 44
form P14 44, 56
form P14/60 44

form P35 44, 56
form P45 54
form P46A or B 41
form SMP1 55
form SSP1(L) 46, 47
form WP1 11, 113
frustrated contract 106
full-time employees 17–18

G

Gardner Ltd v Beresford (1978) 29
genuine occupational qualification
(GOQ) 5–6, 7, 111
good faith, duty of 14–15
gratuities 39
Gregory v Tudsbury (1982) 51

H

Hall (Inspector of Taxes) v Lorimer
(1994) 16
harassment 70–1
*Hayward v Cammell Laird
Shipbuilders Ltd* (1988) 37
health and safety at work 13,
57–69, 76
first aid cover 64–5
infectious diseases 65
liability for employee's stress
level 67–8
medical checks and HIV 65–6
occupiers' liability 66–7

regulations regarding working
environment 61–2
repetitive strain injury (RSI) 63
responsibilities 57–8
smoking policy 68–9
see also Control of Substances
Hazardous to Health;
Management of Health and
Safety; Reporting of Injuries,
Diseases and Dangerous
Occurrences
Health and Safety at Work Act
1974 17, 57–60, 66
Health and Safety (Display Screen
Equipment) Regulations 1992
62
Health and Safety Executive 59,
61, 68, 112
Health and Safety First Aid
Regulations 1981 64
HIV 65–6
Howman & Son v Blyth (1983) 46
HSE *see* Health and Safety
Executive

I

illness, persistent genuine 102
inaccurate information 83
industrial action 79
Industrial Relations Act 1971 96
industrial tribunals 107–10

Industrial Tribunals (Constitution and Rules Procedure) Regulations 1993 108

Industrial Tribunals Extensions of Jurisdiction (England and Wales) Order 1994 108

Industrial Tribunals Extensions of Jurisdiction (Scotland) Order 1994 108–9

infectious diseases 65–6

Inland Revenue 15, 31, 39, 43, 55, 56

insolvency 36

Insolvency Act 1986 36

Institu Cleaning Co Ltd v Heads (1995) 70

Institute of the Motor Industry v Harvey (1992) 54

Institute of Personnel and Development 9

K

Kent Management Services Ltd v Butterfield (1992) 30

L

"last in first out" (LIFO) 85

legal advice and representation 109

liability 66–8

Lipkin Gorman v Karpnale Ltd (1992) 33

M

MA *see* Maternity Allowance

McNally v Welltrade International, T James and Welltrade Middle East Ltd (1978) 28

McSherry and Lodge v British Telecommunications plc (1992) 63

Management of Health and Safety Regulations 1992 60, 62–3

Manual Handling Operations Regulations 1992 61

Marshall v Harland and Wolff Ltd (1972) 106

Mat B1 51, 55

Maternity Allowance 54–5, 112

maternity issues 51–6
   benefits, use of 54
   leave 52–3, 88
   part-time workers 51–2
   records 55–6
   return to work 53
   time off for antenatal care 51
   see also Statutory Maternity Pay

Mears v Safecar Security Ltd (1982) 47

misconduct 94, 96, 101

misrepresentation 28

Misrepresentation Act 1967 1, 28

Morley v Heritage plc (1993) 31

multiple test 16

N

National Insurance Contributions
32, 34, 40–1, 44, 48, 55, 56,
72, 112
nationality 7
*Nationwide Anglia Building
Society v Hooper* 90
NICs *see* National Insurance
Contributions
notice 105
*Nottinghamshire County Council v
Bowly* (1978) 102

O

obedience, duty of 14
Occupational Pension Schemes
(Equal Access to Membership)
Amendment Regulations 1995
42
occupiers' liability 66–7
*Office Angels Ltd v
Rainer-Thomas & O'Connor*
(1991) 104
*O'Kelly and others v Trusthouse
Forte plc* (1983) 18, 41

P

Pape v Cumbria County Council
(1992) 58
Paris v Stepney Borough Council
(1951) 57

part-time workers 17–18, 20, 39,
41–2, 51–2, 88, 98
Patent Act 1977 14
pay and benefits 30–45, 82–3
accrued 83
advances 31–2
authorised deductions 34
average weekly 87–8
board and lodging 32
cash shortages, recovery of
35–6
casual workers 41
equal pay 37–8
holiday pay 31, 33
insolvency 36
itemised pay statement 30–1
minimum wages 44–5
National Insurance
Contributions 40–1
overpayment of wages 33–4
part-time workers 41–2
payment through bank account
34–5
pensions 38–9
personal gifts 39–40
service charges and tipping 43
Sunday trading 42–3
tax implications 40
transport provision 45
unfair deductions 36
union dues collection 45
wages, definition of 30
withholding of 101

see also PAYE; Wages Act

PAYE 34, 40, 43–4, 55, 72, 112

pensions 38–9, 41

period of incapacity for work 47

permits 11

personal gifts 39–40

Personal Protective Equipment at Work Regulations 1992 62

personal relationships within workplace 95

photographs 2

PIW *see* period of incapacity for work

Polkey v A E Dayton Services Ltd (1987) 88

pregnancy 95, 103

   see also maternity

Pregnant Workers Directive 52

profit-related pay scheme (PRP) 31

Protection from Eviction Act 1977 32

Provision and Use of Work Equipment Regulations 1992 61

psychometric tests 8–9

Public Order Act 1986 70, 71

public sector organisations 81

Q

qualifying continuous service for employees' rights 19

R

race 7

Race Relations Act 1976 7, 8, 71

race discrimination 8, 103

Ready-Mixed Concrete (South East) Ltd v Minister of Pensions and National Insurance (1968) 16

Reay v Sunderland Health Authority 54

records 72–3

   maternity issues 55–6

   recruitment 2–3

recruitment 1–11

   advertising 4

   age limits 9

   application forms 1–2

   criminal offence 4

   disabled persons 9–10

   domestic problems 6–7

   genuine occupational qualification 5–6, 7

   indirect discrimination 7

   permits 11

   photographs 2

   psychometric tests 8–9

   records 2–3

   references 3–4

   religious activities 8

   sex and race discrimination 8

   women in the workplace 5

   young people 10–11

redundancy 76, 82, 85–91, 96
   alternative employment 90
   average weekly wage 87–8
   consultation with workforce
      88–90
   continuous employment
      calculation 87
   maternity leave 88
   part-time workers 88
   payments 86–7
   selection of employees 85–6
   time off for job seeking and
      training 91
   unfair selection 86
references 3–4, 28–9, 74–5
Reid v Camphill Engravers (1990)
   36
religious activities 8
religious dispensations 23
repetitive strain injury (RSI) 63,
   112
Reporting of Injuries, Diseases
   and Dangerous Occurrences
   Regulations 1985 63–4, 65, 72
resignation 105
restrictive covenants 104

S

Safety Representatives and
   Safety Committees Regulations
   1977 76

Schmidt v Austicks Bookshops Ltd
   (1977) 22
Schmidt v Spar- und Leihkasse
   der früheren Ämter
   Bordesholm, Kiel und
   Cronshagen (1994) 82
self-certification scheme 48
SERPS *see* State Earnings
   Related Pension Scheme
Servants' Character Act 1792 75
serve, duty to 13
service charges 43
sex discrimination 8, 23, 39, 42,
   103
Sex Discrimination Act 1975 2, 5,
   7, 22, 45, 70, 71
sickness 46–50, 102
   absence on long-term basis
      48–9
   schemes 47–8
   self-certification procedure 49
   single day's absence on regular
      basis 49–50
   see also Statutory Sick Pay
Sim v Stretch (1936) 3
Small Employers' Relief 56
Smith v Safeway plc (1995) 22, 23
smoking policy 68–9
SMP *see* Statutory Maternity Pay
Social Security Act 1975 40–1
Social Security Act 1985 39
Social Security Contributions and
   Benefits Act 1992 47

Sorbie v Trust House Forte Hotels Ltd (1977) 37
special awards 100
Spring v Guardian Assurance plc (1994) 3
Stadt Lengerich v Angelika Helmig (1995) 42
State Earnings Related Pension Scheme 38–9, 41
Statutory Maternity Pay 26, 30, 52, 54–5, 56, 72, 113
Statutory Sick Pay 26, 30, 46, 48, 72, 113
Stevenson Jordan and Harrison Ltd v Macdonald and Evans (1952) 16
stress 66–7
strike action 79
subcontractors 15–16
suing for damages 79, 83
Sunday trading 42–3
Sunday Trading Act 1994 42
suspension 93–4

T

Tarmac Roadstone Holdings v Peacock (1973) 88
terminating contracts 104–6
termination of employment 95
Tesco Stores Ltd v Nattrass (1971) 59
Theft Act 1968 33

theft at work 103
tipping 39, 43
Trade Union and Labour Relations (Consolidation) Act 1990 76
Trade Union and Labour Relations (Consolidation) Act 1992 78, 96, 100, 103
Trade Union Reform and Employment Rights Act 1993 108
trade unions 45, 76–80, 84, 89–90, 95, 103
training and instruction 93
transfer of undertakings 81–4
Transfer of Undertakings (Protection of Employment) Regulations 1981 81, 82, 84, 113
transport provision 45

U

"unilateral variation" clause 26
upper limb disorder (ULD) 63

V

video display units 62

W

Wages Act 1986 30, 33, 34, 35, 36, 44, 107

Wages Councils 26, 44–5

Walker v Northumberland County Council (1995) 67

warning 94

Whittaker v Minister for Pensions and National Insurance (1966) 16

Williams v Watsons Luxury Coaches Ltd (1990) 48

women in the workplace 5

work provision, duty of 12

Workplace (Health, Safety and Welfare) Regulations 1992 61–2

X

X v Commission of the European Communities (1995) 66

Y

young people (under 18) 9, 10–11, 113